HOW TO GET YOUR SECURITY DEPOSIT BACK

HOW TO GET YOUR SECURITY DEPOSIT BACK

A Tenant's Guide

SANDY MEADE

Copyright ©2016 Sandy Meade

All rights reserved. No part of this publication may be reproduced, distributed, or transmitted in any form or by any means, including photocopying, recording, or other electronic or mechanical methods, without the prior written permission of the publisher, except in the case of brief quotations embodied in reviews and certain other non-commercial uses permitted by copyright law.

Published by Crusty Bear Books
Beloit, Wisconsin

website: www.crustybearbooks.com
e-mail: crustybearbooks@gmail.com

Gregory Meade, Editor

First Edition
Printed in the United States of America

DISCLAIMER
This book is designed to provide information in regard to the subject matter covered. It is sold with the understanding that the author and publisher are not engaged in rendering legal or other professional service. If legal or other expert assistance is required, the services of a competent professional should be sought.

Every effort has been made to make this book as complete and as accurate as possible. However, there may be mistakes both typographical and in content. Therefore, this book should be used as a general guide.

The purpose of this book is to educate and entertain. The author and Crusty Bear Books shall have neither liability nor responsibility to any person or entity with respect to any loss or damage caused or alleged to be caused by the information contained in this book.

ISBN-13: 9781945326011
ISBN-10: 1945326018

Library of Congress Control Number: 2016915112
CreateSpace Independent Publishing Platform
North Charleston, South Carolina

CONTENTS

Dedication · vii
The Origin of the Crusty Bear · · · · · · · · · · · · · · · · · · · ix
Introduction: Your Security Deposit · · · · · · · · · · · · · · xi

PART ONE · 1
Chapter 1 The Security Deposit Problem · · · · · · · · · · · · · · · 3
Chapter 2 Why I Can Help You - My Journey· · · · · · · · · · · · ·9

PART TWO· 17
Chapter 3 Protecting Your Security Deposit · · · · · · · · · · · · 19
Chapter 4 How To Move Into Your Apartment· · · · · · · · · · · · 31

PART THREE · 37
Chapter 5 Catching-Up - Starting NOW · · · · · · · · · · · · · · · 39
Chapter 6 Living In Your Apartment· · · · · · · · · · · · · · · · · · ·48

PART FOUR · 49
Chapter 7   How To Move Out of Your Apartment:
            Giving Notice· 51
Chapter 8   Cleaning· ·62
Chapter 9   Repairing Damage· 71
Chapter 10 The Check-Out: Requesting Your Security Deposit · · · · ·77

PART FIVE		**87**
Chapter 11	Getting Your Security Deposit Back	89
Chapter 12	The Decision To Go To Small Claims Court	93
Chapter 13	Going to Small Claims Court	98
	Final Thoughts	105
	Forms	107
	Tenant Resources	115
	About the Author	119
	One Last Thing…	121

DEDICATION

*This book is dedicated to my Mother
who taught me how to see life as an adventure
and, always to follow my own star.*

THE ORIGIN OF THE CRUSTY BEAR

As told to me by my Mother:

One day my nephew David, age five, was spending the day at his grandmother's house. About mid-afternoon the phone rang. An extended family member who was having personal problems called my Mother for emotional support.

While his grandmother talked on the phone, David played quietly in the living room but was within earshot of the phone call. At one point, my Mother, a deeply religious woman, acknowledged the relative's struggle by saying, "Well, I guess that must be your cross to bear."

My Mother said that after ending the phone call and rejoining David in the living room, David asked, "Grandma, what's a crusty bear?"

This is how Crusty Bear was born and has come to symbolize our day-to-day difficulties, hardships, and life struggles.

Sandy

INTRODUCTION

Your Security Deposit

Are you planning on moving soon? Have you lost your security deposit in the past? How will you fit this move into an already busy schedule? And what about your <u>current</u> security deposit?

Moving can be hectic. Don't let your security deposit get lost in the shuffle!

When you lose all or part of your security deposit you feel cheated. When you don't know what to do about it, you feel worse. That's one of the reasons why I wrote this book.

Let me start by saying that your lease agreement is the <u>road map</u> for your tenancy and will be referred to often. It spells out what you agreed to do and when you agreed to do it. This book is a guide or key to help you <u>navigate the road</u>. If you currently do not have a lease agreement you will need to obtain a copy of the lease agreement for the state that you live in. (You may be able to find this online for free.) So, let's start our journey.

I live in the state of Wisconsin. In checking the Wisconsin Department of Consumer Protection website, I found that their most current statistics are from 2014. On the *Top Ten List of Consumer Complaints* landlord-tenant issues are listed as number two. Landlord-tenant problems are not a new issue and they aren't just a Wisconsin problem. Something needs to change.

This book will answer your questions and give you simple (but important) step-by-step instructions so that you get your security deposit back.

I've been a tenant and lost part of my security deposit. And guess what? I didn't like it. But, at the time, I didn't know what to do about it. And then, a few years down the road, my life changed and I became a landlord.

In our early years of owning property, my husband and I owned both single family houses and apartments. We also managed property for other landlords. At one point, we were handling thirty-two units. Over the years we've had our fair share of tenants.

Being a landlord is a learning process and somewhere along the line we noticed that our former tenants would call us when they were looking for a new place to live. There seemed to be a pattern. Tenants would usually live in an apartment for a while and then they would want a single family home.

They would generally call and say, "We're looking for a house now, do you have anything available?" Tenants usually don't come back if they hate their landlord, so, we knew that we were doing something right. We treated them fairly. Since that time, my husband and I have taken different paths in life. He continues to be a landlord and so do I.

Through the years I have learned the issues that can cause security deposit deductions. I will show you how to avoid them. While I know that I can help <u>my</u> tenants, another reason that I decided to write this book is because I know that I can help other tenants as well - tenants that are not mine - and I know that I can help YOU.

This is the book that I needed when I was a tenant. And if you are a tenant, this is the book that you need. If you follow the simple steps, you will be able to make a smooth and easy exit from your apartment and move on to your next home <u>with</u> your security deposit.

THE STEPS TO GETTING YOUR SECURITY DEPOSIT BACK

This is what you will learn:

In **Part One**

- you will learn the purpose of the security deposit and why landlords keep them
- you will learn why I can help you

In **Part Two**

- you will learn when, where, and how to start protecting your security deposit
- you will learn about the importance of your lease, what you need to look for in the lease, and why you need to know it
- you will learn how to begin the process of protecting your security deposit
- you will learn the "Moving In" process, the exact steps you need to take, and when you need to take them

In **Part Three**

- if you are in the middle of your tenancy, you will learn the steps to catching-up so that you can protect your current security deposit
- you will learn the simple steps to protecting your security deposit so that you can live worry free

In **Part Four**

- you will learn the process of "Moving Out" when you find your next home

- you will learn how and when to give your landlord notice that you are moving
- you will learn where tenants get tripped up and the importance of planning your move
- you will learn the difference between "damage" and "wear and tear"
- you will learn when, how, and why you need to demand the return of your security deposit

In **Part Five**

- you will learn why you will hear from your landlord after you move out
- you will learn about the decision to go to Small Claims Court
- you will learn about Small Claims Court

This book will change your life. You don't have to lose your security deposit because you waited too long to protect it. You will learn to understand the process. And you can also be the person who family members and friends come to for help. And when they come to you and ask, "Can you help me (or tell me) how I can get MY security deposit back?" I encourage you to help them. Share what you have learned. Share what you know because there is no shortage of landlord-tenant problems.

The things that you will learn in this book, your landlord already knows. And that is exactly why you need to know them. Understanding the whole tenancy process will make you a smarter tenant. This book will empower you.

Forewarned is forearmed and that means tenants, too. Let's get started.

PART ONE

ONE

The Security Deposit Problem

Let's start by defining some terms and looking at the purpose of the security deposit.

WHAT IS A SECURITY DEPOSIT?

This seems like a silly question. Yet, when I've asked this question, I've been told that it is the amount of money you need so that you can rent an apartment. This is only partially correct. When tenants have only a partial understanding of what a Security Deposit is, what it covers, and why they need one, it only follows that problems will occur.

Security Deposit by definition is this:

> **Security.** This brings to mind two words: safety and protection. If you are planning to rent an apartment then it is obvious that it is the safety and protection of the landlord's property - the apartment - that the security deposit covers.
>
> **Deposit.** This word implies that something is "left" or is "given as a pledge."

The Security Deposit then is money that you leave with the landlord, as a pledge, to ensure the safety and protection of the apartment.

This sum of money is held by the landlord for the term of the lease. Some states require landlords to pay interest on the security deposit while other states do not.

THE PURPOSE OF THE SECURITY DEPOSIT

Most landlords require a security deposit. Besides protection of the landlord's apartment, it also encourages tenants to do all the things that they agreed to do when they signed the lease.

The problem is this: when the tenant signs the lease the full purpose of the security deposit is not always explained to them. If the tenant does not ask any questions about the deposit the landlord may assume that the tenant already knows.

So we actually have a two-fold problem: The landlord requiring a security deposit but never fully explaining the reason to the tenant and the tenant expecting to pay a deposit but never fully understanding why.

As a tenant, you need a clear understanding of what the security deposit covers and why. We will cover this more fully in a later chapter. Briefly, the security deposit covers cleaning, any unpaid rent or bills, and repairs for any damages done to the property. It does <u>not</u> cover "wear and tear" and <u>should not</u> cover a partial payment for your landlord's next vacation.

WHY DO LANDLORDS KEEP SECURITY DEPOSITS?

First, there are the legitimate reasons: to pay for cleaning, any unpaid rent, or bills (like sewer bills), and to pay for the repair of damages done to the property. Then there are the other reasons:

1. **Extra income**

    Some landlords see the security deposit as extra income. Sounds a lot like greed doesn't it? They already have the money (which may be in an interest bearing account) so keeping the deposit is like getting free money with or without interest.

2. **Security deposits are an easy target for abuse**
   Security deposits are easy targets for the landlord to abuse. There is a process to giving notice, "Moving Out" of your apartment, and requesting the return of your deposit. You could get tripped up anywhere along the process if you do not fully understand it.

   Landlords, through experience, understand this process and are able to help their tenant in two ways. One, by giving them a written form with instructions and, two, by verbally telling the tenant their expectations. Unfortunately, tenants don't usually ask for any help and landlords don't always offer.

   The reward the landlord gets for not helping their tenant is to possibly keep the deposit. So there is actually an incentive **not** to help. This is unfortunate for everyone because, with help, many security deposit problems could be avoided altogether.

3. **Tenant inexperience**
   Most states require the landlord to provide a list of deductions made from a tenant's security deposit. When the landlord fails to provide the list or return the deposit, some tenants give up, walk away and never go after their deposit. And this tends to be the case, more so, when the tenant is moving out of the state. When tenants give up and walk away from their deposits this encourages more abuse.

   In my experience, there are many reasons, both warranted and unwarranted, why tenants do not get their security deposit back. Sometimes, tenants do not fully understand their obligations and/or they do not know how to go after their deposit. These are things that we will address.

4. **Tenants are hesitant to go to court**
   When a tenant does not get his full security deposit back and feels like it has been wrongfully withheld he may have no idea what to do. Unfortunately, landlords know this, too.

   While going to court may be an option, tenants may be hesitant to even try.

Going to court can be inconvenient, time consuming and intimidating. Additionally, tenants may have no idea where to start, what to do, or who to even ask. Some tenants believe that they don't stand a chance of winning. When tenants feel unsure and intimidated they are less willing to try to get their security deposit back. Landlords then, by default, play the law of averages and win.

When there is no clear path many tenants start to feel hopeless, like it doesn't really matter what they do, because they won't get their security deposit back anyway. There are many reasons why tenants do not go after their security deposit, but being intimidated by the court system should not be one of them.

ONGOING SECURITY DEPOSIT PROBLEMS

Security deposit problems are not new. In researching this issue, I found that the Wisconsin Department of Consumer Protection began keeping records in 1976. And surprise, in 1976, security deposit issues and landlord-tenant issues were listed as number three on the list of *Top Ten Consumer Complaints*. And while I haven't check the list on a yearly basis, my guess is that landlord-tenant issues have continued to be on this list.

The good news is... there is hope. With the internet and computer access, more and more resources are available to tenants. Tenants are now easily able to research tenancy problems and find suggestions and solutions to those problems. There are also tenant organizations to help tenants as well.

The bad news is... for as far as we have come with easy access to solutions, many landlord-tenant problems still exist. The problems can be diverse and sometimes complicated.

The simple answer is to do your research well, learn and understand the whole rental process, and persist in going after your security deposit if you think that it has been unjustly withheld.

WHY DO TENANTS WORRY ABOUT THEIR SECURITY DEPOSIT?

In a nutshell, for all the same reasons that landlords keep them. If you lost all or part of your security deposit in the past and you don't really understand why, then it would only make sense that you would worry about getting it back in the future. And if you are worried about your security deposit you are wise. But what you need to do now is read, learn, prepare, and turn that <u>worry</u> into being empowered. And that's where I come in.

THE LEARNING CURVE

Trust me when I tell you that the learning process around security deposit issues has been no cake walk, (or no easy task), for me. Seeing the problems and formulating solutions has taken time. It started when I was in my twenties and I was a tenant. Losing part of my security deposit was a real learning experience and it didn't make me happy. Then, by some weird alignment of the stars, I became a landlord.

I discuss my journey more in the next chapter, but let me just say that it has been a learning process. I had to figure out which procedures worked for my tenants and which didn't. Along the way I learned to keep the things that worked and fix or change the things that didn't. This process, for me, has evolved over a twenty-plus-year time frame and I'm still learning. But before we jump in and start the learning process I want to give you some general information.

First, to keep things simple, I will be using the word <u>apartment</u> when talking about your rental unit. The information in this book also applies to a house, a condo, or any living area that you are renting.

Second, while either a male or female can be a tenant or a landlord, I will be using the male gender when I talk about any human being in the book. He is the landlord, he is the tenant, he is the judge… you get the idea. It just makes explaining things easier.

Third, beware of horror stories and do not borrow other people's problems. There are enough ways to lose your security deposit without getting emotionally involved and buying into someone else's problems to help you do it. There are many tenants out in the world who have had security deposit issues. That is why this issue makes the list of *Top Ten Consumer Complaints* on a regular basis!

Everyone has their story. Do not get bogged down, sucked in, or your thoughts swayed by other people's situations. The truth is, <u>not ALL landlords are bad, and not ALL tenants are good</u>. Your situation is unique to you and your landlord. Put your focus on learning the process, empowering yourself, and working to get <u>your</u> security deposit back.

And lastly, in the next chapter I am going to tell you about my journey, how I've come to learn what I know, and how I know that I can help you. If you are planning on "Moving Out" of your apartment within the next two months and need information now, and you want to skip my story, feel free to jump to **Chapter Five: Catching-Up - Starting NOW**. You have a lot to do, and not much time to do it.

After you are all moved and settled into your new place, please come back and read the chapters that you missed. In doing so, you will get the full picture of the rental process. Once you understand the whole process you will know what steps to take, when you need to take them, and you will be able to protect <u>any</u> security deposit that you make in the future.

Next, in Chapter Two, we will look at My Journey and why I can help you.

TWO

Why I Can Help You - My Journey

When I was in my middle twenties I lived with my boyfriend in the Milwaukee, Wisconsin area. We moved several times in a four-to-five-year time span. Each place that we lived was a completely different experience. These experiences were the start of my education about two things: landlords and renting from the tenant's perspective.

THE HOUSE

Our first house was a two-bedroom rental cottage in Pewaukee, one of the suburbs in the Milwaukee area. It was a small, cozy place with no basement. We lived there with my boyfriend's best friend Bob.

We all worked. Life in the cottage was fairly uneventful for the first few months that we lived there. Then one day we didn't have any water. After three days of not having water we found out that the house had a well and something had gone wrong with the pump.

The landlord told us that the motor on the pump had burned out because we were using too much water. In essence, it was <u>our fault</u> that the pump motor wasn't working. I remember thinking, how could that be? Everyone that lived in the house worked and we were gone all day. How much water could we be using? How hard could that poor pump be working? There were NO demands on the pump all day long and doing dishes and taking showers seemed like normal use. We were not washing cars, or watering grass, or filling up a swimming pool, so I didn't quite understand.

So, to be honest, I personally did not know anything about wells, pumps or pump motor's. I didn't know how they worked or how they burned out or why. I also didn't know how we could use so much water that it would cause the pump motor to burn out. After all, isn't that the motor's job? To run the pump? But things wear out. It happens.

This experience turned out to be our first tenant-landlord dispute. We just happened to be the lucky tenants living in the cute little house when the motor for the pump decided to die. Knowing what I know now, it must have been very convenient to blame the tenants... and that was us! The pump motor got old and its untimely death impacted our security deposit.

LESSONS LEARNED

That whole experience made me more aware of how quickly unexpected things can happen. I don't think we could have prevented it. And who – **ever** - in their life, rents a house and asks, "I see you have well water, so exactly how old is the motor for that pump?"

In fact, in my twenty-plus-years of being a landlord, exactly no one has ever asked me that question. I believe that tenants in general want to know that the faucets turn off and on, the water runs, the sink doesn't leak, and that the drain works. So, in my first experience as a tenant, I learned that the landlord is not always right.

THE LARGE APARTMENT COMPLEX

Our next home was at a large apartment complex in St. Francis, near General Mitchell Field Airport. Our main contact was with an on-site rental manager. Upon signing the lease, we got a list of rules. Where to park, where not to park, where to put the garbage, and on and on.

Initially, I was a little concerned about the list of rules. While I was not really a "*rule breaker*" in general, just having a **list of rules** seemed intrusive, almost like someone telling me when to breathe. But the complex had city water, so I knew that there was no chance of the motor on the pump burning out. And if there was a motor somewhere, and it did burn out, the chances were pretty good that we wouldn't get blamed.

As it turned out, the rules were not really intrusive in our lives. We still went to work every day, we lived our lives, and it was actually a nice place to live. The apartment was very modern, the carpeting was new, and we had a balcony. It also had drapes. I remember being impressed by the fact that we had *real drapes*. In all reality, the complex was huge and I can see, now that I look back, that there was a need for some type of structure (rules) for the safety of everyone who lived there.

Lessons learned

Getting our deposit back was not an issue. This was a positive learning experience that was beneficial to my future role as a landlord. It taught me <u>what to do</u>. When we gave our notice to move we received a letter telling us exactly what we needed to do to get our security deposit back. I use this letter, in part, later in this book, in **Chapter Seven: How to Move Out Of Your Apartment: Giving Notice**. This information helped us, and it will help you.

As much as living in this apartment complex was a good experience, here's the rub: when we gave our notice to move we had thirty days left on our lease and we started apartment hunting. We found a cute, two-bedroom upper apartment in an older home. It had a living room, separate dining room, and an eat-in kitchen. It also had hardwood floors and an incredible amount of charm. And even though it was an upper apartment, the steps to get there were indoors. That was a plus.

So, as we packed, cleaned, and prepared to move out of the large complex at the end of the month, there was a knock at the door. It was our new landlord. He came to bring our money back. He said that he had rented the apartment to another couple and he wanted to return our money.

Looking back now, I'm not sure if that was quite legal or not. But one thing that I did know for sure was that as soon as we moved out of our apartment, we were homeless. And this is where the drapes come in. One day we had an apartment with *real drapes* and the next day we not only didn't have drapes, we didn't even have a window. Unless you want to count the car window. It was kind of ironic.

Certainly there was the option of a motel or staying with friends or family until we found a place to live (and we did do that), but those options weren't ideal. And it was somewhat out of desperation that we rented our next apartment in a small complex.

THE SMALL APARTMENT COMPLEX

Our new home, the small complex, was on Farwell Ave near the UW-Milwaukee College Campus. The apartment complex had three levels and about eighteen apartment units total. We lived on the first level. The owner/landlord was an on-site manager and to his credit I believe that he did try to manage it professionally.

Lessons learned

This whole tenancy was absolutely rich with landlord lessons. Unfortunately, many of them I could only see in hindsight and some not until many years later.

This is the place where I learned my first lesson about reading leases. The owner/on-site manager added his own terms to the lease agreement - something I really didn't pay much attention to until we were planning to move out. But let's start with the "Moving In" process first.

When we decided to rent the apartment we met with the manager/landlord to review the lease and get the keys. I really didn't think that this would take as much time as it did. He reviewed the lease, he also went over any and all additional paperwork pertaining to the apartment. Next, he gave us a tour of the building... <u>the whole building</u>. (I kept thinking, is this really necessary?) This ended up being a two-hour process and I can tell you with 100% certainty (and some embarrassment) that I did not listen to a word that he said.

We were in transition and basically homeless. It was already difficult enough to pull myself together in the morning, get to work on time, and work all day. And then there was a certain amount of uneasiness and stress around the whole idea of not knowing exactly where we would be sleeping at night. This whole situation, for me, was already exhausting.

Meeting with the landlord to sign the lease, get the keys, and finally have an apartment was a good step forward for us. However, it was also a painful and excruciatingly long two-hour ordeal. I know that I sat and pretended to listen. I tried not to look desperate or even tired while the whole time all I really wanted to do was move a few things into our new apartment, take a shower, and sleep. And **no**, the apartment did not have drapes. But it did have windows. And at the time, that was a huge step up.

So, what is the whole point of me telling you this story? I want you to start thinking about the idea that it is important to read your lease. Despite anything - <u>any single distracting thing</u> - that was going on in my personal life, it would have been a wise decision to pay attention when the landlord was reviewing the lease agreement. This whole situation will be reviewed again in an upcoming chapter.

So, fast forward to "Moving Out" time. We had lived in the apartment for at least a year. Our lives had become relatively stable. We decided that it was time to move. This time, out of the Milwaukee area. I found the lease agreement and read it to see what we needed to do to move out, in regard to giving notice, cleaning, etc.

I found that most of the terms of the lease were pretty straight forward, lucky for us. But the landlord had added a paragraph stating that the carpets needed to be cleaned. Additionally, he preferred that we rented <u>his</u> carpet cleaning machine to do the job. That was a surprise. But it was also something I would have known if I had paid attention when he initially reviewed the terms of the lease.

It was also a surprise when we got our security deposit back in the mail minus the cost of re-painting the apartment. That was an unfair deduction, and a lesson in itself.

WEARING A NEW HAT

After being tenants for five or six years we moved from Milwaukee to a smaller town and my life changed. Like I said earlier, due to some weird alignment of the stars, we became landlords. Who saw that coming? Certainly not me! This is when the landlord learning curve got steep. I saw the other side of the landlord-tenant relationship. Now I was wearing the landlord hat.

GAINING EXPERIENCE/LEARNING THE ROPES

Experience is a great teacher and learning to be a landlord was not something that just happened overnight. With every new tenant there was something to be learned. Sometimes the worst tenant experiences were also the best learning experiences.

Over time, we could see the problems that tenants struggled with during the rental process. We tried to find solutions, change our forms and address these problems. Sometimes the changes worked and sometimes they didn't. It was all a learning experience.

I learned that the landlord-tenant relationship is a business relationship. (The landlord or rental agent is not your friend.) On some level, it is also an adversarial relationship that you can't get away from. For tenants, there is a lot of fear around the whole security deposit issue.

One **big** thing that I did learn was that tenants do not understand the whole rental process. They don't understand it because no one ever taught them <u>and</u> they are busy living their lives. And really, why would that even be something that would show up on their radar? It is exactly like my situation when we lived in Milwaukee. I didn't care; I didn't want to understand; I just wanted to live my life.

BEING THE LANDLORD

So, now as the landlord, I could see the problem, that tenants didn't understand the whole rental process. I tried to find ways to make their rental process easier. Sometimes I was successful at helping them and sometimes I wasn't. Sometimes they listened and were open to suggestions and other times they resented my input.

With the next tenant I would change my approach, always trying to find the perfect words or create the perfect form, to better help the tenant (and ultimately help us as well). Over the years, I made several changes, I tried several approaches. And finally I figured it out, I needed to write down the whole rental process and make it a step-by-step guide for the tenant.

Truthfully, in all the years of being landlords, we did have some success. Prior tenants would call us when they were looking for a new place to live. Having tenants come back, wanting to have us as their landlord again, was a compliment. We were doing something right. But again, it was always (and continues to be) an ongoing learning experience.

THE TAKE AWAY MESSAGE

In the process of becoming a landlord I have learned that landlords know the game. They know the paperwork and they know their property. When I was a renter all I was doing was living my life. It's very easy to fall into not caring about the security deposit because truthfully, <u>you don't know what you don't know</u>. And, what you don't understand does put you at a disadvantage.

But that's where I come in and is another reason why I wrote this book. <u>I know</u> what <u>you don't know</u>, and I also know <u>what you need to understand</u>. Especially now, because the dollar amounts for both rent and security deposit continue to rise; meaning that, you have even more money to lose.

When it comes to your security deposit, you may feel like your landlord is holding all the cards; like he has power over you. But the truth is this, the landlord only has power to the extent that you do not understand the rental process and your rights. This book will help level the playing field.

PART TWO

THREE

Protecting Your Security Deposit

Getting your security deposit back is really a game called "Before and After." And it all comes down to this: if you want to increase your chances of winning the security deposit game you need to play the game well and protect your deposit.

WHEN, WHERE, AND HOW THE PROTECTION STARTS

When to start protecting your security deposit.

You went apartment hunting. You finally found an apartment that is cute, cozy, and fits your needs perfectly. You submitted your application and it was approved. Now you must meet with your landlord or rental agent for the building to sign the lease and get the keys.

Bingo... Horns... Bells... Whistles... Whatever it takes. Protecting your security deposit starts <u>now</u>... so pay attention. The minute that you sign the lease and pay the security deposit is also the minute that you should start protecting it.

Where to start protecting your security deposit.

A tenancy is usually in one of three stages: before, during, or after the tenancy.

1. **The Before stage:** You haven't moved in yet.
   In an ideal world you would be able to read this book and understand the whole process before you need it. At this point, you may be thinking about getting your own place or you have been looking and are close to making the decision to rent. Understanding how to protect your security deposit before you even rent an apartment will definitely be to your advantage.
2. **The During stage:** You are currently renting.
   In reality, everybody lives somewhere. Perhaps you are thinking about moving. Or your lease is ending and you are considering your options. Or you have already decided to move and you may be anticipating trouble getting your current security deposit back.

   While you are not starting from step one, you **are** still living in the apartment. This is to your advantage. So, there are still things that you can and should do so that you can avoid problems and protect your security deposit. If this is you - see Chapter Five.
3. **The After stage:** You already moved out.
   If you moved out of your apartment, returned the keys and learned that you will not be getting your security deposit back, you're probably angry. And you want help NOW! You may be thinking that there isn't a lot that you can do.

   Trying to get your security deposit back 'after the fact' is a lot more difficult. Your success is going to depend on how strong of a case you can pull together. Unfortunately, it may just end up being a learning experience; a lesson in how to do it differently next time.

   So, the simple answer of where to start protecting your deposit is this: you start wherever you are NOW.

How to start protecting your security deposit.
When you meet the landlord or rental agent for the first time, the following things will happen:

1. You will sign the lease.
2. You will sign other paperwork, like smoke detector or pet agreement forms.
3. You will pay the rent and security deposit.
4. You will get the keys to your new apartment.

When you leave this meeting you should have the following:

1. <u>A receipt for rent and a receipt for the security deposit</u>. Some landlords combine the amounts and will give you one receipt. If your landlord gives you a receipt that covers both rent and deposit, make sure that the receipt clearly identifies the amount paid for rent and the amount paid for the security deposit. If you are paying by check, make a notation on the check itself and identify each amount.

    The other option is to write separate checks, one for the deposit and the other for the rent. I would never recommend paying cash for either rent or security deposit. If it is your only option, be extra careful to keep those receipts in a safe place.
2. <u>Keys</u>. The landlord may give you either one or two keys. Note how many keys the landlord gives you because that is the number of keys you will be expected to return.
3. <u>A signed copy of your new lease agreement and other paperwork</u>. Let's start with other paperwork:

<u>Other Paperwork</u>
This may include additional agreements that you negotiated with your landlord like an agreement to allow you to have a pet or an agreement to do repair work or cleaning in place of a security deposit. In addition, and depending on your city or state regulations, you may have paperwork regarding the smoke detectors and carbon monoxide detectors in your

apartment. With any additional paperwork, just make sure that you read and understand what you are signing and that you are given a copy of everything that you sign.

The Lease
The subject of leases could be a book by itself. I recommend that you read every word in your lease. For the purposes of this book, I am going to cover the important points in a typical lease form that pertain to your security deposit. There may be a few landlords who do not use a written lease form, but in general, when you rent an apartment, a lease is required.

LESSONS LEARNED
In my life as a tenant, and then as a landlord, I have negotiated many many leases for both houses and apartments and this is what I have learned.

As a Tenant
I remember meeting with the landlord to sign the lease, pay the rent and security deposit and get the keys to the new apartment. If you read "My Journey" in Chapter Two, this would be the Small Apartment Complex that I am talking about.

When my boyfriend and I sat down at the landlord's kitchen table he brought out forms and started talking. He talked about the building and safety, the rules and the lease... and it went on and on and on.

Then we got a tour of the building... the <u>whole</u> building. It was more than two hours later when we finally left the meeting with the keys and could start moving into our new apartment.

I remember thinking, *Oh, my God, I can't believe that took so long.* At the time, the only thing I learned from that experience was that it takes a while to get the keys.

As a Landlord
So, fast forward to the time when we became landlords. We are the ones choosing tenants and setting up the meetings. I am the one reviewing and

explaining the lease and the other paperwork to the new tenants. This is how the experience looks from the other side of the table.

First, let me just say that whenever we had an apartment for rent there were generally several people interested in renting it. This was more so the case if we had a house available. So, to be the ones chosen to rent the apartment, the potential tenants were generally thrilled. They showed up at the meeting excited to sign the lease, get the keys, and to be able to start "Moving In."

Initially, I sat down with the tenants and explained any safety issues and reviewed the paperwork. I tried to hit the important points in the lease because I felt that the tenants needed to understand what they were agreeing to. The lease, after all, is a legally binding contract.

For me, the process became routine. The paperwork was the same (give or take a form or two), and giving the "lease speech" was the same. After reviewing the lease with several different tenants, I could talk about all of the forms by just glancing at them once or twice. At some point, and maybe it was just out of boredom (because I was giving the same lease speech over and over), I started noticing the new tenants' facial expressions.

While I was telling them about all of this <u>VERY IMPORTANT</u> information I could see that their eyes were glazing over. And that is when I got my '*Ah ha!*' light bulb moment. It finally dawned on me. <u>They are not even listening.</u>

And, on some level, I believe that tenants do think that this paperwork is probably somewhat important, but, on another level, they don't really care. They are just listening because they have to and their main goal is to move into the apartment.

Reflecting on all of this, it was very easy to go back to when I was the tenant. Which made the whole 'glazed eyes' phenomena easier to understand.

LOOKING BACK

Renting isn't an easy process. I remember we looked at several apartments before we found one that we really wanted. And the reality is, we weren't the only ones looking. Even when we filled out the rental application there was no guarantee that we would be selected. So, while we waited on one landlord to get back to us we still had to keep looking at other apartments.

So, actually finding a place that we liked and having the landlord approve our application was exciting and a big relief. We could stop looking and start planning to move. The meeting then, to pay the deposit and rent, was really the last big step. I remember feeling happy and relieved (and a whole bunch of other emotions, if you read my story) because the worst of the renting process was now over and we could finally get the keys, move into the apartment, and get on with our lives.

When we met with the landlord and he started talking, the only thing that I was thinking about was moving into the apartment. We had the week-end to do it, so my thought was: *Just give us the keys.* And it really isn't too big of a jump to understand that my new tenants were probably thinking the same thing.

So, I get it. Lesson learned here. But the take-away message and important thing that I want you to understand is that your lease is a binding legal agreement. Since you are bound to the terms of the lease, it is a good idea to find out what you are agreeing to. So READ THE LEASE and do your best to listen when you meet your new landlord. Yes, it is boring. No, you don't want to be there, but listen anyway.

As a little incentive, pretend that if you don't listen, and you don't understand the lease that you will lose your security deposit, because it just might happen. So, set aside your excitement and the anticipation of moving and focus on this last BIG step before you move in.

THE LEASE

With my tenants I use the WISCONSIN STATE LEASE AGREEMENT. I prefer using this form because it covers the legal statutes about renting and will contain terms that are in the best interest of both the landlord and the tenant.

Some landlords have their own homemade lease form. I believe that in the past these lease forms were easier to read than the state forms. However, over the years, the state forms have become more consumer-friendly and thus, have become easier to read and understand.

The concerns I have about landlord homemade forms are that they may contain clauses that only benefit the landlord and some clauses may even be illegal. In a perfect world this would not happen, but this is planet Earth, so beware.

If you do not live in the State of Wisconsin, find the lease form online that is specific to your state. Buy a copy if necessary, and read it. Let me repeat that:

Find the lease form online that is specific to your state. Buy it if necessary, and READ it.
You will be miles ahead understanding exactly what's in the lease form before you meet your landlord and sign a lease. When you do meet to sign paperwork, I recommend that you listen carefully, even though it's boring stuff. If anything seems questionable, ask yourself this: Is this fair and reasonable to both the landlord and me? And if there is anything about the lease (or any of the paperwork) that you do not understand, **Ask questions.**

What you will find in the lease about your Security Deposit.
Looking at the Wisconsin State Lease Agreement there are a number of things that you will find that pertain to your security deposit. Some are related to "Moving In," which we will cover now, and others that pertain to "Moving Out," which we will cover in a later chapter.

The Lease Agreement will contain the following/or similar wording:

1. **Security Deposit** (or may be **Damage Deposit**.) Upon execution of this Lease Agreement, Tenant shall pay a deposit in the amount of $_____to be held by _____. Receipt of the deposit is hereby acknowledged by Landlord as security for any damage caused to the premises during the term of the lease. Landlord may place the security deposit in an interest bearing account and any interest earned will be paid to Landlord or Landlord's representative. If the person holding the deposit is a licensed real

estate broker acting as an agent the Security Deposit will be held in the broker's trust account.

What this means/what is important to remember

The Laws vary from state to state, but the Security Deposit or Damage Deposit clause should state the amount being paid and who will be holding this money. Some states require landlords to tell tenants the bank name and branch where the money is held. If the money is in an interest bearing account, the individual state laws also determine exactly who will receive payment of the interest earned when the lease/tenancy ends.

When you meet with the landlord and pay a security deposit be sure that the correct dollar amount is written on your lease agreement. It is also important to know who will be holding the deposit and exactly what your state laws are regarding the payment of interest on your deposit.

2. **Condition of Premises**. Tenant has examined the premises and that they are at the time of this Lease in good order, repair, and in a safe, clean and inhabitable condition. Tenant has 7 days after the beginning of the lease term to notify the landlord in writing of damages or defects to the premises.

What this means/what is important to remember

There may be nicks to the woodwork or cracks or holes in the wall that you did not notice when you initially saw the apartment. Or maybe the exhaust fan in the bathroom doesn't work but you didn't flip on the switch so you didn't notice that either. This particular part of the lease is encouraging you to protect your deposit. It is saying: you have seven days to tell your landlord (in writing) what's broken in your apartment so that you won't get charged for the repair when you move out.

While some tenants think that this is a good idea, in reality, most tenants never get around to informing their landlord of any defects. Truthfully, I think that most tenants just wanted to get settled and live their life. And maybe that is how you feel, too. But the bottom line here is this: your lease is telling you, you have seven days, and this is a step you can take to protect your security deposit. We will cover this again in Chapter Four as we get closer to "Moving In."

Back to the lease:

3. The landlord will give the tenant a written description of any physical damages charged to the previous tenant's security deposit as soon as such description is available.

<u>**What this means/what is important to remember**</u>

If there were any damages charged to the previous tenant's security deposit it is in your best interest to find out what they were. Since the lease states that the landlord will give you a written description of these damages you definitely want this information. Although you are obviously entitled to get this information, in reality you may be the one to have to pursue it. That's okay. This will be covered in Chapter Four.

PROTECTING YOUR SECURITY DEPOSIT - THE FIRST STEPS

Protecting your security deposit involves keeping all of the important papers regarding your tenancy together. The first step then is to get a large manila clasp envelope, thirteen by ten is a good size. Take a bold or bright colored marker and write SECURITY DEPOSIT/TENANCY on the envelope.

After you meet with your landlord, take the TENANCY CHECKLIST form (a portion of which is shown below). Date the listed items when you receive them and put them in your envelope. DO IT NOW. The reality is, these papers have to be somewhere. Don't set them down and shuffle them around and risk losing them or having them accidentally thrown away. Put them where they belong while they are in your hand. Stuff them in the envelope and you are done with them for now.

Partial form: <u>Tenancy Checklist</u>

TENANCY CHECKLIST

Date each item as you place it in the envelope with this checklist

_____ 1. Keys (number of keys received) _____
_____ 2. Rent receipt
_____ 3. Security deposit receipt
_____ 4. Lease Agreement
_____ 5. Other Agreements or paperwork: _____

You will be adding things to your envelope throughout your tenancy so put your envelope in a safe but nearby place. These first baby steps toward protecting your deposit are easy and take very little time. But don't let this fool you into thinking that these steps are not important. Trust me, they will save you time and energy down the road.

Frequently Asked Question: What if I didn't pay my Security Deposit by Cash or Check?
Sometimes tenants agree to do work instead of paying a cash security deposit. This can be a good arrangement for both the landlord and the tenant. If you agree to do work in exchange for the security deposit or part of your rent, you need to have it documented. Some printed lease forms have an area called 'Special Conditions' (or a similar name) this would be a good place to add a short explanation of the work you are doing in exchange for the rent or security deposit.

Your other option would be to create a written form about this agreement. You need to document the main points of what you are agreeing to do. And the agreement should be signed by both the landlord and you, the tenant. See the example on the next page.

Repair Agreement

Date_____

Jim Brown, tenant at 107 Green Street, Delavan, Wisconsin, agrees to do the following list of repairs at the rental address in exchange for the $600.00 security deposit.

1.
2.
3.

The landlord agrees to obtain / pay for the materials and the tenant will provide the labor.

The repairs will be completed by _____.

_____   _____
Tenant   Landlord

Recommendation

My recommendation would be to create a separate document that covers all the important points of your agreement. You don't want any misunderstandings about who will be doing the work, what work will be completed, when it will be completed, and who will be paying for the materials.

If you agree to make repairs for part or all of your rent or for your security deposit, place a copy of the agreement in your envelope.

SUMMARY

1. Protecting your security deposit starts when you pay the security deposit.
2. Protecting your security deposit starts wherever you are NOW in your tenancy.
3. Protecting your security deposit starts with keeping all your rental documents together, in a safe place, in a manila envelope.
4. When you leave the meeting with your landlord you should have copies of everything that you signed.
5. State Lease Agreements cover terms that are in the best interest of both the landlord and the tenant.
6. Your lease should state the amount of security deposit paid.
7. Your lease informs you that you have seven days to document any damages.
8. Your landlord must inform you of damages charged to the previous tenants security deposit.
9. Create and keep a detailed written copy of any additional agreements with your landlord.

If you have followed the steps up to this point, you've just made a good start at protecting your security deposit. You've done everything that you can for now, and you are ready for the next step, moving into your apartment.

FOUR

How To Move Into Your Apartment

1. Open the door.
2. Move your belongings in.
3. Close the door.

It sounds so simple. Could it be that easy? Yes, I suppose it could be. But the goal here is to protect your security deposit. As we learned in the last chapter there are still two important steps you need to take before you are free to settle in and enjoy your life and your apartment. So, let's go through the "Moving In" process and see how it's done.

"MOVING IN"

The difficult part of finding an apartment is over. At this point, you have probably met with your landlord, signed all of the paperwork, have the keys and are ready to move in. Let's talk about the two simple, but important steps that you still need to do to protect your security deposit.

Step One
By now you should have read your lease. You know that you have seven days, after the start of your lease, to inspect your new apartment and inform the landlord about anything that is either damaged or defective (meaning, not working properly). <u>Step One is accomplished by completing the Check-In Procedure.</u>

Step Two
The lease also tells you that the landlord must give you a written description of any physical damages that were charged to the previous tenant's security deposit. This is important information for you to know. <u>Step Two is accomplished by checking the box on the Check-In form or by asking your landlord.</u>

THE CHECK-IN PROCEDURE
The Unfurnished Apartment
When you arrive at your new apartment and find it clean and in good repair as promised, you can start moving your things in. Both Steps One and Two (from above) can be accomplished by completing the Check In Procedure. There is a Check-In Checklist in the back of this book. It is to your advantage to complete this form.

With that being said, it has been my experience that most tenants do not complete a Check-In Checklist or do any type of Check-In Procedure. In my twenty-plus-years as a landlord, I have had exactly ONE couple complete a Check-In Form and return it to me. And that was more than fifteen years ago.

In the past, doing a Check-In Form was a tedious task. Tenants were asked to go through their new apartment slowly and note the condition of each room. Including the insides of closets, cupboards, and drawers. It is not surprising that no one ever completed the form.

With advances in technology, there are high-quality cameras available on most cell phones today. You can document the condition of your apartment accurately in pictures, thus creating a baseline history for your apartment. Taking pictures makes this whole process easy and fun.

Recommendation
I recommend that you go through your new apartment slowly. Complete one room before moving on. Progress in a logical manner so that the pictures are grouped my room or area. Take pictures of any damages or defects that you find. They can be as simple as a crack in the wall, a nail hole, chipped trim, or a missing shelf in the medicine cabinet.

Check everything carefully because you are assuming the responsibility for the care and condition of the apartment. Keep in mind that whatever you do not find on the way in you may pay for on the way out which could be in the form of a security deposit deduction.

Example
I have an acquaintance (he was never a tenant of mine), who lost his security deposit at his last apartment and he was not happy about it. At his new apartment, he took more than two hundred pictures of the current condition and gave his new landlord a copy of all of the pictures on a flash drive.

So, back to your apartment. In addition to the pictures, you can also use the paper Check-In Checklist. If you find any damage just make a notation on the form to see the pictures on the flash drive. Pictures are an easy and fun way to document the condition of your apartment. And remember, every picture is worth a thousand words.

THE FURNISHED APARTMENT
The Check-In Procedure for a furnished apartment is similar to that of the unfurnished apartment. If the apartment you rent includes any furnished items, the landlord should give you a complete and detailed list of all the furnished items. Check your apartment to be sure that you have all of the items on the list. If the landlord doesn't give you a listing of furnishings, then make your own list. Again, pictures are a good idea. This is especially

true with furniture because furniture will not get better looking with either age or wear.

DESCRIPTION OF DAMAGES
According to your lease agreement, in Wisconsin, your landlord must give you a written description of any physical damages that were charged to the previous tenant's security deposit. You definitely want to know this information. Although you are obviously entitled to get this information, in reality, you may have to ask for it. The easiest way to accomplish this is to combine this request with your Check-In Checklist.

When your landlord sends you the list of damages charged to the previous tenant's deposit make sure that you take pictures of the damaged areas. If you have them on a flash drive, put it in your envelope. In addition, make a notation on your Check-In Checklist (the form in your manila envelope) of the damaged area and where the pictures are located in case you need them. This will help you avoid being charged for damages that you did not do.

See the combined Check-In Checklist/Damage Request Form on the next page.

HOW TO GET YOUR SECURITY DEPOSIT BACK

CHECK-IN CHECKLIST/DAMAGE INFORMATION REQUEST

Address of Rental Unit: _____
Name of Tenant(s): _____
Move-In Date: _____

Please check the condition of the following items within seven (7) days of tenancy:

- stove
- sink
- toilet/tub/shower
- light fixtures
- walls and woodwork
- doors
- ceilings
- windows
- floors
- carpeting

Please note the general condition of the apartment and let us know about any damage or problems that we should be aware of.

Damage Information Request
☐ I/we request a list of physical damages or defects that were charged to the previous tenant's security deposit.

_____   _____
Tenant signature   Date

SUMMARY

1. You have seven days to do the Check-In Procedure.
2. Document the condition of your apartment using a Check-In Checklist and pictures.
3. Do an inventory of any furnished items, making your own list if the landlord does not provide one.
4. Give your landlord a copy of the Check-In Checklist and Damage Information Request.
5. Put a copy of your Check-In/Damage Information Request form and pictures (flash drive) in your manila envelope (or make a notation where the pictures are located).
6. When the landlord sends you a list of the damages charged to the previous tenant's deposit, take pictures of these areas and put them in your manila envelope (or make notations of where the pictures are located).

Once you have done the Check-In Procedure you can relax and breathe. These are very simple but important steps. Your hard work is now done. It is safe to settle into your apartment and live your life.

PART THREE

FIVE

CATCHING-UP - STARTING NOW

If you been with me since the beginning of the book, then you have already taken a number of steps to protect your security deposit. You now have the choice to read this chapter and review the steps you've already taken or you may skip this chapter because you are already prepared.

This chapter was specifically written for the tenant who has been living in their apartment for awhile. If this is you, then my guess is that you have not done everything that you should do to protect your deposit. And, at this point, you may be thinking about moving or may have already found your next new home. Either way, if this describes you, then this is where you start.

You need to cover your bases and get organized. Especially if you are anticipating having any problem with your landlord returning your security deposit. In fact, if this <u>is</u> the case, then you are very wise to prepare now. While it is never too late to start protecting your security deposit, there are specific steps that you have missed and for you, this is your catch-up chapter. So, let's get started.

THE STEPS TO CATCHING-UP

First of all, you need a place for all of your paperwork. I recommend that you get a large manila envelope. A thirteen by ten clasp envelope is perfect. Then look in every drawer, cupboard, cabinet, and closet and gather all the paperwork that you can find regarding your tenancy. Before you moved into your apartment you probably signed a lease. Find it! Also locate any security deposit and rent receipts as well as any other documents that you may have signed with your landlord.

Use the following tenant checklist (which is also available in the back of the book). Go down the list item by item. Check off the items you have by dating each listed item when you put it in your envelope.

TENANCY CHECKLIST

Write the date next to each item as you put it in the envelope.

_____ 1. Keys (number of keys received) _____
_____ 2. Rent receipts
_____ 3. Security Deposit receipt
_____ 4. Copy of Lease Agreement
_____ 5. Copy of list of charges made to the last tenant's deposit
_____ 6. Smoke Detector Agreement
_____ 7. Carbon Monoxide Detector Agreement
_____ 8. Check-In Form
_____ 9. Other _____

KEYS

If you have been living in the apartment for a while you may not know the exact number of keys that you were given. Don't try to fake it. If you can't remember, it is better to just leave the space blank or write down 'currently have two keys' (or however many keys you have). Another option would be to ask your landlord how many keys he gave you. Because, the truth is, the landlord does know how many keys he gave you and he most likely has it documented. And this would also be the number of keys that your landlord expects you to return when you move out.

RENT RECEIPTS

Take your rent receipts and put them in order by month with the most recent month on top. Then paper clip or staple them together, record them, and put them in your envelope.

Frequently Asked Questions

In the process of teaching people how to protect their security deposit, I am often asked the following questions regarding rent receipts:

I want my security deposit back, not my rent. Why do I need to keep rent receipts?

If your landlord tries to deduct unpaid rent from your security deposit your rent receipts will prove that you <u>did</u> pay your rent. They are legal proof.

Is it really important or necessary to keep rent receipts?

Yes, and No. If you paid your rent with cash, **yes**. Your receipt is the only way you can prove that you actually paid your rent. If you paid your rent by check, **no**. Your check is your receipt. But if you find rent receipts put them in your envelope anyway. They have to go somewhere and it doesn't hurt to keep them. Receipts not only show that you paid your rent but **when** you paid it. The receipts speak to your rental history and your level of personal responsibility.

What if I can't find all of my rent receipts?

In all reality, if you are paying your rent by check you already have a receipt. If you are paying your rent with cash and you can't find receipts that are five or six months old it is not that critical. The truth is, if you haven't paid your rent for five or six months (even if you do pay with cash), chances are pretty good that your landlord would have addressed this issue a long time ago and you probably would have been evicted. Your goal here is to protect your security deposit, so, if you are paying with cash, the most recent rent receipts are the most important.

At this point, you <u>are</u> still a tenant, and you are playing catch-up. So, starting today and moving forward each and every time you pay your rent, get a receipt and put it in your envelope. And just a note to those tenants who do pay by check. If you are planning on moving soon I recommend that you go to your online banking site and make a copy of your most recent rent check and put it in your envelope.

If check copies are available online do I still need to make a copy?

Yes, but just the most recent rent check. If you are planning on moving soon you want to get your ducks in order now. You do not want to be scrambling around making copies in the middle of your move. So, suck it up and make the copy now. Put it in your envelope. You will have enough to do at "Moving Out" time. Think of it as another baby step (or for you, a catch-up step). Just do it!

I pay my rent by check. So, why do I need to keep the receipt?
Because if you're given a rental receipt it has to go somewhere. Certainly you can throw it away or burn it, but, besides being a receipt, it does show your history of on-time rental payments. It shows that you are a responsible person. It is just easier to keep the receipt right now than it is to try to find a copy of your check later.

SECURITY DEPOSIT RECEIPT

Very bluntly here, if you cannot prove that you paid a security deposit how will you ever be able to get it back? The truth is, you may not be able to. It would all depend on your landlord's honesty. I said this earlier in the book and it does bear repeating. If this chapter is your starting point, you need to hear this. And if you have been with me since the beginning of the book, it will not hurt you to hear this again:

Your landlord is not your friend. Period.

He may be nice or even kind. He may even be someone you've known all of your life. It doesn't matter. Owning property and being a landlord is a business. The relationship you have with your landlord is a professional/business relationship. People do not become landlords to make friends.

I have tenants that I like very much. They are very nice people and, had I met them under different circumstances, there is a possibility that we would have become friends. But once people become tenants of mine, friendship is not an option. At least not while they are tenants.

So, back to you. Your landlord has legal obligations to you. He needs to make sure that the apartment that you are renting is tenable, meaning that you can safely live there.

You landlord needs to make sure that your furnace works in winter and that you have hot and cold running water as well as working drains. Additionally, you need a safe electrical system, and doors and windows that both lock and function properly. So, in thinking about it, does any of this describe a friendship? **No!**

Back to your Security Deposit receipt. Find it! Put it in your envelope. If you need to go to your online bank site to print a copy of your canceled check for your security deposit, do it. Get it done. Because this is all about your security deposit and getting it back.

COPY OF YOUR LEASE AGREEMENT

With rare exception, when you rent an apartment, most landlords will require a lease agreement. The lease agreement is a legally binding contract that describes the terms and conditions of your tenancy, including your legal obligations.

Hopefully, in your search for paperwork you found the copy of your lease agreement. If you cannot find it, ask your landlord for a copy. While this isn't the ideal situation, it **is** still a good option. The reality is, life is busy, things get lost and that includes lease agreements. But you still need a copy. So, if you cannot find it, ask your landlord. Once you either find or obtain a copy of your lease agreement, READ IT.

Question: What if I don't have a written lease?
Even if you don't have a written lease agreement there are still tenant-landlord laws in your state that apply to your tenancy. And at this point, it is important to know what the laws are and how they apply to you. Get online and search for: (name of your state) State Lease Agreement. Print a copy of your state's Lease Agreement and READ IT.

When you start reading the lease form you will probably notice that it is a long and boring form. It's dull, dry, and at times confusing. This would probably be a great read if you had insomnia. And while you may very well have insomnia, the actual point of you reading the lease is because you have a landlord. The lease describes your agreement with your landlord. You need to know what you agreed to.

I don't know how *readable* lease agreements are in other states, but I do know that Wisconsin has made big improvements in their Wisconsin State Lease Agreement. It has become more consumer-friendly. So that everyday people, like you and me, who are not lawyers, can understand it better when we read it. At this point, read the lease and learn what you can about your rental agreement. Some parts of the lease, those pertaining to your security deposit, will become more important at "Moving Out" time.

LIST OF DAMAGES

In some states, landlords are required to give their new tenants a list of damages that were charged to the previous tenant's security deposit. Read your lease agreement to see if your landlord is required to give you a list of deductions made for damages.

In the long run, knowing this information can only help you. If the previous tenant was charged for a stain on the carpeting, then the landlord can't charge you for the same stain when you move out. Ask your landlord for the list of damages charged to the previous tenant's security deposit.

CHECK-IN

When you rent an apartment, generally you are only given seven days at the beginning of your tenancy to report any defects or damages that you find in your new apartment. Since you are coming late to the game here, you can't go back and do a Check-In Form and give it to your landlord.

But you <u>can</u> do the Check-In Form for your personal knowledge. Now is actually a good time to complete it. You will learn the current condition of your apartment. And you may find problems that need to be addressed, either by fixing them yourself or by contacting your landlord (see **Chapter Four: How To Move Into Your Apartment**).

OTHER FORMS

Depending on where you live it is possible that you have signed other agreement forms. I have heard of agreements that cover parking issues (where you <u>must</u> park your vehicle) to garbage issues (where you <u>must</u> put your garbage). On some level, I think we have gone a little wild with all the paperwork. But in general, these forms tend to cover safety and security issues that effect all the tenants in a building or complex. Which is probably a good thing.

I recommend that you do an inventory of any furnished items in your apartment. If your landlord did not provide a list of these items, then make your own list. Keep a copy in your envelope.

Other forms that I personally use include a 'Smoke Detector Agreement' and a 'Carbon Monoxide Detector Agreement.' Your landlord may use these forms as well. In searching for paperwork regarding your tenancy, if you find any other forms that you negotiated with your landlord, put them in your envelope. List the name of the form on the Tenancy Checklist.

SUMMARY

1. Protecting your security deposit starts wherever you are NOW.
2. Protecting your security deposit starts with gathering all your tenant-related documents.
3. Find and keep your rent and security deposit receipts (especially if you paid with cash).
4. If you cannot find a copy of your Lease Agreement, ask your landlord.
5. Ask your landlord for a copy of the damages charged to the previous tenant.
6. Ask your landlord for copies of any agreements that you cannot find.

Catching-up is never easy, but it is important. At this point, you still have the advantage of living in the apartment. In the long run, it is easier to catch-up now, even in baby steps, than it would be when you are trying to pack and move.

Once you have completed the Tenancy Checklist you can relax and breathe. You have covered the important steps to protecting your security deposit.

SIX

Living In Your Apartment

At this point, you've done everything that you can to protect your security deposit and the information is safely tucked away in your manila envelope.

As you live in your new home, continue to put your rent receipts in your manila envelope, especially if you are paying your rent with cash. If you make any repairs or improvements, take before and after pictures. Down the road it will show that you not only took care of the apartment but that you made improvements.

Settle into your new home.
Live your life.
Sit down, put your feet up, breathe...

...come back to this book when you are ready to move out.

PART FOUR

SEVEN

How To Move Out of Your Apartment: Giving Notice

There is no trick to "Moving Out" of an apartment.

Anybody can do it.

"Moving Out" **and** getting your security deposit back, now that can be a bit more challenging. For many tenants the "Moving Out" process goes like this:

1. You decide to move.
2. You find another apartment.
3. You give your landlord a 30-Day Notice.
4. You move your belongings out.
5. You return your keys and expect to get your security deposit back.

When you do all of these steps and then your security deposit is not promptly returned, or is returned with multiple deductions, it is annoying and frustrating. You feel cheated. And if on any level you felt that the landlord was a friend, you also feel a little betrayed.

The path to getting your security deposit back can be full of twists and pitfalls. In the next four chapters you will learn how to maneuver the path and avoid the pitfalls. Because how you move out of your apartment plays a big part in the eventual return or <u>non-return</u> of your security deposit.

Let's begin:

Once you make the decision to move it is time to find your manila envelope. This is the envelope that contains the receipts, your lease agreement, and all the other paperwork pertaining to your tenancy. This is the moment that you have been preparing for all along.

When you find your manila envelope, open it and pull out your lease agreement. If you are one of the rare tenants who does not have a lease agreement with your landlord, then you should already have a copy of the general lease agreement for your specific state. Remember, even if you did not sign a lease, there are still laws in your state that apply to your tenancy.

By this point, you should have read your lease and have somewhat of an understanding of the laws that apply to your tenancy. Today is the day you need to look at them more closely.

DEFINING YOUR LEASE TERM

Your lease is your road map. When you make the decision to move you need to know exactly when your lease term will end. Read your lease agreement and find the paragraph that defines your lease TERM. The TERM of your lease will tell you <u>when the lease started</u> and <u>when it ends</u>. The date that the lease ends is the date that you will complete your legal obligation of the lease agreement and you can move.

EXAMPLES
#1
Let's say that your lease started on June 1, 2017 and it ends on May 31, 2018. Today is April 15, 2018. You just completed your taxes, you

filed online and you know you are going to get a bunch of money back. You decide to pay off some old bills with the money. When you pay off the old bills you find that you have more money available each month. Nice!

Your two-bedroom apartment has been feeling a little cramped for a while so you decide to find something with three bedrooms. It is time to move.

Reading your lease confirms exactly what you thought. Your lease ends on May 31, 2018. Now would be a good time to start looking for your new apartment. You have enough time to find a new place and let your landlord know that you'll be moving at the end of your lease term.

Let's look at another example:

#2

Your lease started on August 1, 2017 and it ends on July 31, 2018. Today is April 22, 2018 and the IRS was incredibly fast at sending your tax refund. You paid off those old bills and you still want a larger apartment. You go out looking and you find a new apartment with three bedrooms, and you can afford it.

Reading your lease, you find that your lease term ends on July 31, 2018. Now what? Can you move?

The truth is, yes, you can move. Your landlord cannot make you stay. But if you move out early you are not completing your obligation to the lease agreement.

So, certainly there would be some type of consequence for this decision. You may have to pay for advertising to find another tenant, and, worst case scenario, if a suitable tenant is not found, you may be liable for the rent on the remaining months of your lease.

There is also the possibility that you could lose your security deposit. So, while your landlord cannot make you stay you want to think about the possible outcomes and decide wisely if "Moving Out" early is worth what it will cost you.

RECOMMENDATION

I recommend that you do not create any problems for yourself. You can stay in your current apartment, save your money (don't let that refund burn a hole in your pocket!), and find a new apartment closer to the end of your lease term.

The best case scenario would be to complete your lease obligations. The whole point of this book is to help you get your security deposit back and that is exactly why the <u>end date</u> of your lease term is so important. If you want to move, it is in your best interest to do so when your lease ends.

MONTH-TO-MONTH TENANCY

If your lease term ended and you are still living in your apartment your rental agreement has probably converted (or changed) to a month-to-month tenancy. This happens automatically if you do not negotiate a new lease with your landlord. If your Wisconsin tenancy is on a month-to-month basis, you are only required to give (at least) a 30-Day Notice when you decide to move.

THE 30-DAY NOTICE

The purpose of the 30-Day Notice is to inform your landlord that you plan to move out of your apartment. The Wisconsin State Lease Agreement specifically states that you need to give your landlord (at least) a 30-Day <u>written</u> notice.

EXAMPLE

This is an example of a 30-Day Notice from a tenant. Rick and Sherry were prior tenants and I talked about them in an earlier chapter (without actually mentioning their names). This is the couple who were the <u>only tenants</u> to ever do the Tenant Check-In Form. But fast forward to their "Moving Out" time. Rick and Sherry decided that they wanted to move and Sherry dropped off their 30-Day Notice. <u>Word for word, this is exactly how the notice read.</u>

Mike Meade

Rick & I are giving you our 30 day Notice that we are Moving out of 802 ½ Vine in a week.

Rick & Sherry XXXXXXX

I actually still have the original note. There is a certain amount of humor to it. At the time, it was such a surprise that I just kept the note. So, from this example, clearly you can see this is not a 30-Day Notice.

MY REALITY

In my world, I have found that the whole "giving notice" process works more like this:

My tenants generally sign a one-year lease. I know <u>when</u> their lease ends and so does my tenant. So close to the end of their lease term tenants will either talk to me when they pay their rent or send me an e-mail or text me with a simple message like one of the following:

'My lease ends in September, but I'm not planning on moving yet.'

'I know my lease ends in June, but I'm planning on moving closer to the end of September.'

'Our lease ends in May and we plan to move.'

I will always respond and acknowledge receiving their e-mail or text. If none of this happens and I do not hear from my tenant, I will contact them, because I want to know what their plans are when the lease ends. Communication is key.

YOUR 30-DAY NOTICE
It is time to talk about YOU giving notice.

1. You looked at your lease and you know your lease end date **OR** you are on a month-to-month tenancy and can end your lease anytime with (at least) a 30-Day written notice.
2. You checked your lease and your landlord did not restrict you to giving notice on a rent-paying date.
3. You found another apartment - your future home. Let me just say that you don't have to find another apartment before you move, but some people like to know exactly where they are going before they give notice.

But, new home or not, you are ready to give your 30-Day Notice and move. Now is the time to go back to your lease agreement, to the section that talks about terminating your tenancy.

When you read your lease one of the first things that you will find is that you are required to give the landlord notice of your intention to move. If your tenancy is month-to-month in Wisconsin, then (at least) a 30-day <u>written</u> notice is all that is required.

MY EXPERIENCE
Earlier I talked about my tenants touching base with me towards the end of their lease. The following are examples of exactly how my last three tenants gave their 30-Day Notice.

1. One tenant gave me a sixty-day verbal notice. On December first she said that she and her husband bought a house, they would be moving, and they would be out by January thirty-first.
2. Another tenant gave me notice on June tenth, actually by text and e-mail. She said that she and her family would be moved out by September first.

3. The third tenant gave me a verbal warning (is the best way I can put it) at the beginning of February that the family intended to move. She said that she didn't really know <u>when</u> they would move yet, she thought maybe in about two months.

At the beginning of March, I was told verbally that they weren't going to move yet. At the beginning of April, I was told the same thing.

At the beginning of May, I was told verbally that they would be moved out by the middle of July, but that they would pay rent until the end of July because they would still be there cleaning. And I did get a text message close to the end of July that they were all moved out, the apartment was clean, and that they would be bringing me the keys.

THE TAKE AWAY MESSAGE

So, what does all of this mean? I don't know how the 30-Day Notice requirement is handled with other landlords. But I do know this: unless your name is Steve E. or Tiffany B., <u>I am not your landlord</u>. And I would <u>never</u> recommend that you <u>ever</u> send your landlord a text giving your 30-Day Notice.

The Wisconsin State Lease Agreement is very specific about this. It states that if you want to end your tenancy (terminate your lease) and move, you must provide your landlord with a written notice (at least) 30 days before you want to end the lease.

Please notice that it says written...WRITTEN.

And at the end of the paragraph in the Wisconsin State Lease Agreement, it repeats this again by saying:

Time is of the essence for proving notice of termination (strict compliance with dates by which notice must be proved is required.)

This one sentence is a little cryptic. But it means that the thirty-day time frame is <u>extremely important</u>. *When* you give notice is important. If you end up in court you will need to <u>prove</u> that you gave a 30-Day Notice. And the best way to do that is to *give a notice, get the time frame right,* and *give your notice in <u>writing</u>*.

THE EXCEPTION

With every rule there is at least one exception. This is also the case when giving a 30-Day Written Notice. Unfortunately, written lease agreements have not kept up with the advancements in our technology. Today, in our world, the most popular methods of communication are by e-mail and text message. So, in the tenant-landlord relationship, we need to bridge the gap between what the lease requires (a 30-Day Written Notice) and our current methods of communication (text and/or e-mails).

This can be accomplished by adding either an addendum (additional paper agreement) to your lease agreement or by adding it to your lease at the time you negotiate it. It can be a brief sentence that states that you and your landlord agree to Electronic Delivery of Documents.

BACK TO MY TENANTS

So, as I said above, I would never recommend that you ever send your landlord a text giving your 30-Day Notice to move unless you have an agreement with your landlord for Electronic Delivery of Documents.

Technically, you could argue that a text message is in writing, but if you ever end up in court, do you really want to hand the judge your phone to prove that you gave a 30-Day Notice? And how would you handle it if your landlord told the judge that he never received your text message?

Keep in mind, your landlord is not your friend. Your relationship with your landlord is a legal business arrangement. Keep the relationship business-like.

How I select tenants is another chapter for another book, but very briefly, Tiffany B. is a tenant because she is a responsible person and she works hard. She is also a parent, has a lot of energy and a touch of spunk.

Steve E. is a tenant because he is responsible person as well. He is a parent, a really decent person and a Veteran. He served our country, that was a tipping point for me.

But bottom line here, Steve E. and Tiffany B. are not my friends. I like them, or I would not have rented to them, but they are not my friends. With that being said, if they choose to give me their 30-Day Notice by text, I am okay with that because the thing is this - I know that I am not going to go to court and tell the judge that my tenant did not give me a 30-Day Notice.

But, I am not YOUR landlord. I cannot speak for your landlord or even predict what he will say if YOU go to court. My goal here is to help you protect your security deposit. So, make sure that your 30-Day Notice is <u>written</u> or that your lease includes an agreement to use Electronic Document Delivery.

ABOUT 30-DAY NOTICES

We have just discussed that <u>when</u> you give your 30-Day Notice is important. But <u>how</u> you give notice is important as well.

Some people like to avoid talking to their landlord. Others are just plain uncomfortable telling their landlord face-to-face that they plan to move. If you are a good tenant, certainly your landlord will hate to lose you. But tenants coming and going are all a part of the business.

If you plan to mail your 30-Day Notice either by regular mail or by certified mail all I can say is: <u>don't</u>. That is a lot of unnecessary work. Give your landlord your 30-Day Notice when you pay your rent. If you staple a copy of your notice to the rent check there will be no way that he can miss it. And there will be no misunderstanding of exactly <u>when</u> you gave notice.

Additionally, this will give you the opportunity to ask about your security deposit and it gives your landlord the message that you want your security deposit back. You can also ask him if he has any specific forms to follow or other requirements at "Moving Out" time. By asking these questions you may get some helpful information on what your landlord expects.

SAMPLES OF 30-DAY NOTICE TO LANDLORD

Simple 30-Day Notice:

30-Day Notice of Intent to Vacate Premises

Date: _____

This is my 30-Day Notice that I will be vacating the premises at 191 Bell Street, on or before October 31, 2018.
 The apartment will be left clean, in good condition and I will remove my personal possessions. I will return the key on or before October 31, 2018.
 My forwarding address is: 700 East John Street, Markesan, Wisconsin 53946
 If you have any questions you may contact me at 608-555-1212

Frank Smith

_____

Simple 30-Day Notice with Demand for Security Deposit:

30-Day Notice of Intent to Vacate Premises

Date: _____

Address: _____

This is my 30-Day Notice that I will be vacating the premises on or before October 31, 2018. I am giving you the proper notice that is required by our lease agreement.
 The apartment will be left clean and in good condition. I will remove my personal possessions and I will return the key on or before October 31, 2018.

I would like my security deposit back as soon as possible because I will need it for my new apartment.

The forwarding address for the return of my security deposit is: 700 East John Street, Markesan, Wisconsin 53946

If you have any questions you may contact me at 608-555-1212

Sincerely,

Frank Smith

....

This example is simple and gets right to the point. It tells your landlord:

- I am moving.
- I have given you proper notice.
- I'll clean the apartment and move my things out.
- I will be out by October 31, 2018.
- I want my security deposit back.
- Here is where you can send it.
- Here is my phone number if you need to call me.

SUMMARY

1. Read your lease.
2. Learn your lease end date.
3. Find your new home.
4. When you decide to move, give (at least) a 30-Day <u>Written</u> Notice unless you have an Electronic Document Delivery Agreement.

In Chapter Eight we are going to look at Cleaning.

EIGHT

Cleaning

Now that you have given your 30-Day Notice to move, it is time to start thinking about cleaning. Much like the previous step of giving notice, the cleaning aspect is also addressed in your lease. Read the section of your lease that talks about cleaning. If you do not live in the State of Wisconsin, refer to the lease agreement for your state.

The Wisconsin State Lease Agreement addresses cleaning in the section entitled Security Deposit:

under <u>Deductions,</u>

(4) Landlord may deduct reasonable charges from the security deposit for costs of cleaning, deodorizing, and repairing the Property and its contents for which Tenant is responsible.

It is *one* sentence in *one* part of the lease. It would be easy to skim past it or miss it entirely. Additionally, because it is just addressed in one sentence it almost gives you the impression that it isn't that important, but trust me, it is. Cleaning is a HUGE issue when it comes to you getting your security deposit back.

Now we know that the Wisconsin State Lease Agreement is wide open to interpretation. Let's move on to examples:

EXAMPLES OF "MOVING OUT" LETTERS
#1
This letter is informative. When you decide to move and get a letter like this from your landlord you may be more inclined to believe that your landlord will give your security deposit back. This letter tells you step-by-step what the landlord expects you to do. It is the letter that we received when we moved out of the large complex in Milwaukee. It has been included as a general guideline because you may never get a letter like this from your landlord.

_____

Dear_____

Moving time is always a busy time and you will have a lot of things on your mind now that you have given notice that you are moving. One of the things undoubtedly will be how to get your deposit back. In your case the amount of your deposit is $_____.

Contrary to what some tenants believe, we want to return your deposit and we will return your deposit to you as long as you leave your place "reasonably clean and undamaged." That's what your rental agreement says and that's what we will do. You're probably wondering what "reasonably clean and undamaged" means. So we'd like to tell you how we interpret it and also tell you what you should do to get your deposit back.

Reasonably clean to us means as clean as you would leave your dwelling if you knew your best friend or your favorite aunt were going to move in after you. To get it that clean we expect you to clean the appliances, stove hood, cabinet under the sink both inside and out, remove all non-adhesive shelf paper, use an appropriate cleaner on the showers, tubs, toilets, sinks, mirrors and medicine cabinets. Dust the baseboards, window sills, closet shelving and ceilings for cobwebs. Wash the kitchen and bathroom walls and spot clean the walls in other rooms. Wash the light fixtures and windows inside and out. Vacuum the floors, scrub the floor tile or linoleum. Sweep the entry, patio, stored enclosures and garage. Remove all of your personal belongings including clothes hangers and cleaning supplies. And dispose of all trash. Please DO NOT clean the draperies, shampoo the carpets or wax the floors. We prefer to do those cleaning chores our self and you will not be charged for doing them.

Reasonably undamaged to us means that items which we have supplied should not be missing including light bulbs. Things that we have supplied should not be missing or broken. There should be no burns, cracks, chips or holes in the dwelling or any furnishings. The paint on the wall should be sufficient to last at least 2 years from the time they were last painted. Please do not remove anything that you have attached to the walls or ceilings without first talking to us and please try to avoid nicking the paint in the halls or doorways as you move things out. After you have returned the keys we would like to inspect your dwelling with you to check it for cleanliness and damage and unless we have to get prices on special work or replacement we will refund all deposits owed to you at that time.

We expect you to have moved out completely by_____ because we are making arrangements for new tenants to move in soon after your move out date. We would appreciate hearing from you immediately if your moving plans should change.

We hope your move goes smoothly and we wish you happiness in your new home.

Sincerely,

The Management

_____

#2

This is another example of a letter from a landlord regarding the security deposit and leaving the apartment clean and damage free.

....

Dear _____(Tenant)

We received your 30-Day Notice and we understand that you will be moving soon. According to the terms of the lease, you are required to leave the apartment in a clean and damage-free condition in order to receive a full refund of your security deposit.

    Completing the following list before the end of your lease term will help you restore the apartment to its prior condition and help you get a full refund of your deposit.

_____ Empty and clean the interior of all cabinets, closets, appliances and storage units.
_____ Clean all appliances and fixtures, inside and out.
_____ Clean all ceilings, walls, windows and doors, and flooring of the property.
_____ Remove all nails and screws from the walls and fill all holes with an appropriate compound.
_____ Remove all stains from carpets. Shampoo carpeting.
_____ Remove all personal belongings from the property.
_____ Dispose of all food, trash and unwanted items. Removing them from the property.
_____ Cut the grass.

Please complete all of these tasks by date: _____

_____(Landlord)

....

REGARDING CLEANING

Unless you moved into your apartment under unusual circumstance, it was probably clean when you moved in. When you signed the lease, you agreed to leave the apartment clean when you move out. So, it is important that you fulfill your part of the lease agreement.

The truth is this, if you do not clean your apartment, the landlord will or he will hire someone to clean it for him. In either case, <u>you</u> will pay for it. And trust me, it will cost you more money than you will ever think that it's worth.

The key here, for you, is to find the documents (in your manila envelope) relating to the condition of the apartment when you moved in. This would be your Check-In Checklist and the pictures that you took when you moved in. These two items will give you a good idea of what your apartment needs to look like when you move out. You have thirty days, so now is a good time to start planning ahead.

PLANNING YOUR MOVE

From the examples given above, regarding cleaning, I would say that the information from the Wisconsin State Lease Agreement is probably the least helpful. The form letter from the Management of the large housing complex is the friendliest. And the letter, in checklist form, was the most useful, but not as extensive as it could be.

You have thirty days. Plan the next thirty days so that they include sorting, packing, pitching, and donating items. This is a great time to get rid of things that you do not want, need, or use. Have a garage sale. Remember, your trash may be someone else's treasure. Donate and recycle. Be brutal. If you don't use it, get rid of it, or it will become clutter/junk at your new home. Plan ahead, work ahead, and try to clean and pack the things that you can during the month. It will make your move easier.

THE TIME FACTOR

In my experience, people tend to underestimate the amount of time and energy that it takes to move and clean. This is not so much a tenant thing as it is a human thing. It's also Murphy's Law:

Everything takes longer than you think.

There is a very good possibility that moving will take longer than **you** think. Which can leave little to no time for cleaning. This will impact your security deposit. As one landlord told me: "I think tenants get so desperate at the end… they run out of time and energy, and they end up leaving a mess."

You only have so much time and energy, so waiting until the last minute to clean is not a good plan. The best way that I can help you is by giving you some cleaning tips.

CLEANING TIPS

Your apartment will need a thorough cleaning. These are the tips that I have gathered from friends, family, my tenants, and in researching cleaning tips. Anything you can do in advance to save your time and energy will be worth the effort.

PACK AND CLEAN FROM LOW TRAFFIC AREAS TO HIGH TRAFFIC AREAS

Start with closets and bedrooms. Moving to the higher cabinets or shelves in the bathroom and kitchen.

CLEAN FROM TOP TO BOTTOM

On a room-to-room basis, check light fixtures for dust or damage. Make sure that the light bulbs are working. Move to the ceilings and walls, looking for cobwebs and dirt.

Time Consuming Items

1. The Stove
   The top, sides, front and interior of the stove take a bit of time to clean. I recommend tackling this project a week or two before your moving date.
2. The Refrigerator
   Cleaning the outside of the refrigerator will be the easy part. Defrosting the freezer and cleaning the inside will be more work. You want to do this in advance so that you don't to have to deal with pieces of ice falling all over the kitchen floor on your moving day. Melting ice on the floor is not only a safety hazard, but it will serve as a constant reminder of <u>one more job</u> you must accomplished that day.

   Cleaning both the stove and refrigerator can be time consuming. Remember to clean <u>under</u> both appliances. I have heard about landlord's charging fifty dollars per appliance to do the "under the appliance" cleaning. Planning ahead will make your moving day and your life easier.
3. The Bathroom
   The best cleaning method is usually the easiest and safest and it goes without saying that any fixture that has regular care will be much easier to clean. Since the bathroom is a high traffic area you may have to pack and clean this room the day you move out.

Quick check items

1. Doors
   Check both the front and back of doors. Also check <u>door knobs</u> and the <u>switch plates</u> on the walls because they attract dirt.
2. Light bulbs
   Make sure that all the light bulbs are working; replace them as needed.

3. Windows
   Wash them. It won't take that long. This is a task you can assign to an older child or teen.

   Also remember to dust the window sills, I have been told that landlords have charged forty dollars for "dusting window sills." Don't let this happen to you.
4. Drapes
   Drapes are not generally a big issue, but do spot check them for dirt. Ask your landlord if he has a preferred way for you to deal with the drapes.

SPECIAL CARE ITEMS

1. Carpeting
   If the landlord provides any carpeting, he will expect you to take care of it. First, vacuum the carpet and then check for any spills, stains, or dirt spots. Next, check your lease to see if shampooing the carpet is required.

   If the carpet looks really worn, then no carpet cleaning machine in the world will be able to do miracles and bring the dead carpet back to life. This is the carpet to shampoo and get a picture of yourself doing it. As a tenant, it is your job to take care of the carpet and keep it clean, but it is not your responsibility either to replace it or make a sizable contribution towards new carpeting when you move out.
2. Furnishings
   If your apartment is furnished, find the 'Furnishings Check-In List' that you were either given or created when you moved in. You should also have a good set of "Moving In" pictures.

   Look at your pictures and check the basic condition of the furnishings. Next, decide what you need to do to leave them in the same condition when you move out. Pay special attention to anything that either looks beat-up or was in bad condition when you moved in. In reality, the condition of old carpeting or old furniture will not improve with either age or use.

UTILIZING FRIENDS/FAMILY

If you have family and friends willing to help you move, have your moving boxes and cleaning supplies ready. Delegate tasks; it will make your day easier.

SUMMARY

1. Read and understand what your lease says about cleaning your apartment.
2. Use your Check-In Checklist and set of "Moving In" pictures to guide your cleaning.
3. "Moving Out" is a big job. Plan ahead.

In Chapter Nine we are going to look at Repairing Damage.

NINE

Repairing Damage

Damages are best defined as loss when property is destroyed or injured.

Damage can happen in the process of everyday living. Especially if you have children and/or pets. Kids do things for no reason other than they are just kids. I actually had a child who took a hammer and pounded holes in a bathroom door.

Why would a child do that?

Who knows, maybe he saw his dad pounding things and he wanted to try it out. The point is, damage happens. If it happens by accident - or not - if you are responsible for the apartment, then you need to fix the damage.

YOUR LEASE AGREEMENT

Read the section of your lease that talks about damages. By now, finding this information in your lease should be no surprise. My hope is that you are beginning to understand exactly how important your lease agreement is and how fully it covers <u>all</u> aspects of your tenancy. Again, if you do not live in the State of Wisconsin, refer to the lease agreement for your state.

The Wisconsin State Lease Agreement addresses damages in the section entitled Security Deposit

under <u>Deductions:</u>

(4) Landlord may deduct reasonable charges from the security deposit for costs of cleaning, deodorizing, and repairing the Property and its contents for which Tenant is responsible.

There are thousands and thousands of dollars deducted from tenants' security deposits each year for cleaning and damages, yet the Wisconsin State Lease Agreement addresses these issues in *one* sentence. The thing is this: it is not the responsibility of the State of Wisconsin (or your state) to tell you how either to clean or repair damages. At this point, you just need to understand what your lease says about these items.

The Wisconsin State Lease Agreement basically says this: the landlord may deduct the costs for repairs if you are responsible for the damage.

HOW DAMAGE EFFECTS YOUR SECURITY DEPOSIT

If you are responsible for any damages to your apartment and you do not make repairs, then your landlord can use your security deposit money to make the repairs.

DAMAGES

Now that it is "Moving Out" time, you need to walk around your apartment and look for damages. Some items will be very obvious, like a broken window, a hole in the wall, holes that your dog dug in the yard, or a missing drawer handle that your child pulled off. Own up to the damages and fix them.

Take good before and after pictures of whatever you are repairing. Document any repairs that you made. Keep receipts. Making the repairs will show that you have been a responsible tenant. And it will be cheaper for you to do the repairs than it will be for the landlord to hire someone.

THE DIFFERENCE BETWEEN "WEAR AND TEAR" AND "DAMAGE"

Wear and tear is the natural wearing out or aging of things. It is the result of everyday use. Carpeting is a good example. Carpets begin to show wear patterns and will appear as matted down.

Another example is paint. Paint on the walls and ceilings will eventually begin to chip, crack, or fade. The material that drapes are made of will fade and weaken as a result of hanging in the sun every day. These things are *wear and tear*.

Damage goes beyond *wear and tear*. Like rips or stains in the carpet, or spots of pet urine. When carpets wear out they do not get stains or spots of pet urine. When paint on the wall or ceiling begins to age and fade it does not cause holes in the wall. And dirt on drapes is not the result of fading or weakening of the material. *Damages* are things that are out of the ordinary. See the difference?

THE PROBLEMS WITH "WEAR AND TEAR"

1. **What actually is "Damage" the tenant believes is "Wear and Tear."**

   The real meaning of *wear and tear* is not always understood and it can cause tenants to lose either part or all of their security deposit.

   Example

   I had a couple who gave their notice to move. They moved all of their belongings out of the apartment at the end of the month, but they did not clean or repair anything. When I inspected the apartment and pointed out the dirt and damage, I was told that it was *wear and tear*. Whatever I found in the apartment was just the result of them living there.

They assign everything from fingerprints on the walls, cigarette burns in the carpet, burned out light bulbs and grease on the stove to *wear and tear*. After all, that happened in the course of everyday living... it must be *wear and tear*.

Remember that *wear and tear* is <u>inevitable and acceptable</u> but a worn carpet does not develop cigarette burns. That is *damage*. Grease on the stove is not *wear and tear*. That is dirt. Scum and dirt in the bathtub and shower are not *wear and tear*. That is also dirt.

Accidents do happen, but accidents are not *wear and tear*. Window glass does not wear out. It falls out or it is broken out, but it is not <u>worn out</u>. And the fingerprints, smudges and film on the windows are NOT the result of what happens with age and use.

2. **What is actually "Wear and Tear" the landlord believes is "Damage."**

A new tenant of mine told me that his previous landlord had deducted one-hundred dollars from his security deposit for cleaning the carpets. He said that he had not only cleaned the carpets but he had done a good job. The carpet was just worn.

I said this in Chapter Eight, and I will say it again, there is no carpet cleaning machine in the world that will bring a dead carpet back to life. This is an unfair deduction and the tenant should challenge it.

In Wisconsin, landlord-tenant issues consistently appear on the Wisconsin Department of Consumer Protection's *Top Ten List of Consumer Complaints*. Landlords have been accused of charging tenants for such things as repainting walls when the walls have not seen new paint in years. And replacing the carpeting in the whole apartment because of a couple stains. These deductions are expensive, unwarranted, unfair, and should be challenged.

3. **What is actually "Wear and Tear" and what is actually "Damage" can sometimes be a fine line.**

This whole issue would be easy to understand if an item were considered to be either damaged or undamaged. However, that is not always the case.

Consider these examples:
A door frame may have been rotten in places but it had not actually fallen apart until the tenant kicked the door in. Is this *wear and tear* or *damage*?

A tenant offered to paint the apartment for the landlord and then proceeded to paint every room pink with purple trim. Is this *damage* or *wear and tear*?

A few small nail holes in the wall can be considered *wear and tear*. But, what if some holes are large and some are small and there are one hundred holes? Is that *damage* or *wear and tear*?

What if two switch plate covers are broken? Is that *damage* or *wear and tear*?

What if eight switch plate covers and six outlet covers are broken? Is that *damage* or *wear and tear*? The actual number of anything that is broken does make a difference.

OTHER CONSIDERATIONS

There is also the issue of time. Have you lived in your apartment for six months or for four years? It does matter. Time and regular use can cause any item to become worn. Sometimes there is such a fine line that it is difficult to say if it is *damage* or *wear and tear*.

Often times, it is a combination of both *damage* and *wear and tear*. This is one reason why security deposit cases end up in court. The landlord and tenant disagree and the judge must decide. This is as it should be.

What does all this mean?
It means that you need to have a good understanding of the definition of *wear and tear*. Because your landlord may very well make deductions from your deposit that are unwarranted and unfair.

SUMMARY

1. Repair any damages that you caused during your tenancy.
2. You need to having a good understanding of the meaning of *wear and tear*.
3. If deductions were made from your security deposit for damages that you think are really *wear and tear*, you can challenge these deductions.
4. Even if it is a fine line, and you and your landlord disagree, you still have the right to challenge the deductions. Remember, landlords are not always right.

In Chapter Ten we are going to look at Requesting Your Security Deposit.

TEN

The Check-Out: Requesting Your Security Deposit

Moving day arrives. Ready or not, here you go...

Today is moving day and by now you should have a plan in place. If you've been with me up to this point, you have done some sorting, tossing and already have some boxes packed and ready to go.

The steps of the "Moving Out" process will be the <u>last</u> steps you take to protect your security deposit. These last steps are just as important as the first steps.

YOUR LEASE AGREEMENT

Read your lease agreement. Again, this should be no surprise. You need to see exactly what your lease agreement says about "Moving Out" of your apartment. If you do not live in the State of Wisconsin, read the state lease form for your state.

The Wisconsin State Lease Agreement addresses the "Moving Out" process in the section entitled **Surrender of Premises**:

Upon the expiration of the term hereof, tenant shall surrender the Premises in as good a state and condition as they were at the commencement of this Wisconsin Lease Agreement, reasonable use and *wear and tear* thereof and damages by the elements excepted.

This basically means that when the lease expires, you will move out and leave the apartment in as good of a condition as when you moved in except for *wear and tear* and damages caused by the elements (or Mother Nature).

You gave notice and planned to move. So while the lease states that you will *surrender* the apartment, it really just means that you will be moving your belongings out, and giving the apartment back to the landlord. Which was your plan anyway.

"MOVING OUT" AND YOUR SECURITY DEPOSIT

As you complete your "Moving Out" process you will be taking your final steps to protect your security deposit. In my experience, this is the point where many tenants get tripped up because they run out of both time and energy before the moving and cleaning process is complete. But we discussed this, and today you have a plan.

YOUR MOVE

Move all of your belongings out of the apartment as well as any storage area provided. All of your belongings means **everything**. If you leave personal items behind your landlord may charge you for the cost of disposing of them. That includes any garbage bags. After you are done moving, you can finish your cleaning and do a final check of the apartment. When everything is done, complete the Tenant Check-Out form.

THE TENANT CHECK-OUT FORM

The Tenant Check-Out Form is similar to the Tenant Check-In Form and serves the same purpose, which is to document the condition of the apartment. This time, it is when you move out.

Look at your Tenant Check-In Form and the pictures you took when you moved in. Now walk through your apartment and visually compare your pictures to the condition of your apartment.

If you find that there is nothing else to fix or clean, then complete your Tenant Check-Out Form. This is also the time to take another complete set of *Check-Out* pictures.

I recommend that you take the exact same set of pictures that you took when you moved in. The "Moving In" (before) and then the "Moving Out" (after) pictures will tell a story... this is how the apartment looked when I moved in... and this is how it looks now. If you find areas where you have actually improved the appearance of the apartment, make a note of it on your Tenant Check-Out Form.

The goal here is to protect your security deposit. Remember that a picture is worth a thousand words and it will clearly show that you took good care of your apartment and that you made improvements.

DAMAGES CHARGED TO THE PREVIOUS TENANT

If you were able to obtain a list of damages that were charged to the previous tenant, then take pictures of the listed items. You did not cause this damage. Taking pictures will show that, whatever the damage was, it has not become worse because of you or your tenancy.

FINAL INSPECTION

In some states, landlords are required to inform their tenant that they have the right to be present for the final inspection. While it is not a bad idea, it is not required in the Wisconsin State Lease Agreement. With all of that being said, if you decide that you would like to be there, talk to your landlord.

Set up an appointment. Just make sure that the apartment is ready and that you are prepared. Do your own Tenant Check-Out Form and take your pictures <u>before</u> your final inspection with the landlord.

<u>In my experience as a tenant</u>, we were present at the apartment complex in Milwaukee when the apartment manager came to do the final inspection. We were in our mid-twenties and I had no idea exactly how the process would work. But it actually went very quickly. The manager went room-to-room checking to see that the apartment was clean and undamaged. The whole inspection took under five minutes. He said, "It looks fine," and he left. Our full security deposit was refunded.

<u>In my experience as a landlord</u>, I have not had any tenants ask to be there for the final inspection. Having the landlord and tenant do a final inspection together is an idea that is much better in **theory** than it is in practice.

At "Moving Out" time, tenants are so involved in the moving process they are not thinking about doing a check-out with their landlord. Rather, they are trying to figure out how to get the washer and dryer out of the basement and onto the truck. And when they are finally done moving, they just want to leave the keys behind and not look back.

RETURNING THE KEYS

Returning the keys to your landlord is an <u>important</u> step. Look at your Tenant Checklist to make sure that you are returning the exact number of keys that you were given. If you do not return all of the keys the landlord may charge you for changing the locks.

Additionally, the landlord may consider your actual move out date to be the date you return the keys. Which means that you could get charged for additional days of rent. Returning the keys is a sign that you are all moved out, and that you are gone from the apartment <u>forever</u>.

There are a number of ways that you can return the keys to your landlord:

1. You can leave the keys in the apartment.
2. You can drop the keys off at your landlord's house.
3. You can do a final inspection with your landlord returning the keys at that time.

I have received the following text messages:

'I'll be out by the 31st and I'll leave the keys on the counter'
'We will be out by next week Wednesday and I'll drop the keys off to you'
'The carpets are being cleaned on Thursday and we'll be all done on Saturday.'

While the last text does not specifically mention the keys, they were on the counter and the message was clear. The tenant was done on Saturday.

I am comfortable with my tenants returning the keys in whatever manner works best for them. The truth is, when tenants move, they want to move out, return the keys, and be done. And most of the time returning the keys is not an issue. But for the sake of your security deposit, you want all of your bases covered. So, when you return the keys is important.

Leaving the keys in the apartment is probably the easiest and what most tenants do. If you plan to do this, inform your landlord. If you plan to ask your landlord to be present for the final inspection, you can return the keys at that time.

If you do not want to be present for the final inspection, my recommendation is to drop the keys off at your landlord's house. This will give you an opportunity to talk to him and give him a written request for your security deposit. Call or text ahead, let your landlord know that you would like to drop the keys off.

LETTER DEMANDING YOUR SECURITY DEPOSIT

I think the title **Demand Letter** is old terminology. In doing research, I found that this terminology was born out of necessity. In the past, when tenants did not get their security deposit back they would take their landlord to court. In court, the landlord would say that the deposit was not returned because the tenant did not ask for it. The Demand Letter was then created to request the security deposit and eliminate the landlord's excuse for not returning it.

A demand letter is basically a request that your landlord return your security deposit. You can find several examples of a *"Demand Letter"* on the internet. Some of them are quite formal and others even a bit threatening.

When you return your keys, I recommend that you give your landlord a letter requesting the return of your security deposit.

Example: <u>Letter Requesting Security Deposit</u>

October 31, 2018

Dear _____ (landlord)

Per our lease agreement, I have given you a 30-Day Notice. I moved all of my possessions out of the apartment at _____ (address) as of the above date.

I left the apartment clean and in good repair. When you inspect the apartment if something is not as clean as expected, or you believe that there is damage, I would like the opportunity to remedy the situation.

I am returning ____ keys with this notice.

If you have any questions or concerns you can contact me at this number: _____

My new address is: _____

I would like my security deposit returned as soon as possible so that I can use it at my new apartment.

Sincerely,

_____ (tenant)

QUESTIONS

Do I need to give my landlord a demand/request letter for my security deposit?
Yes, and No. In Wisconsin, the responsibility for the return of a security deposit has shifted from the tenant having to ask for it, to the landlord being required either to return it or account for it. But do read your lease, because it is still important for you to know exactly how your state handles the return of your deposit.

Since our goal here is to protect your security deposit and get it back, it is a good idea to give your landlord a demand/request letter for your deposit. Doing this lets your landlord know that you do want your security deposit back as soon as you can get it. After all, it is your money.

I cleaned the apartment and the landlord said the stove needs to be cleaned. I don't want to go back and clean it, do I have to do that?
Again the answer is Yes and No. I would say Yes! do it, for a couple of reasons.

First, on "Moving Out" day you have 101 things on your mind. It would be very easy to forget to wipe up the muddy footprints from the floor or even the grease from the side of the stove. Offering to fix anything that you forgot says that *No One is Perfect*. And if you were tired and pressed for time, who knows what you forgot.

Additionally, it makes you look good, like you care. And maybe you don't care about the apartment or even care about the landlord, but you

<u>do care</u> about your security deposit. So, your offer to correct things is an easy way to make yourself look good. It shows your good faith effort to move out of your apartment and leave it like you found it, except for *wear and tear*. And that is why you should do it.

If you need another reason, consider this. The landlord is letting you know that the stove is not as clean as he expected it to be. This is pretty much a heads-up to you, that if you don't clean it, he will, or he will hire someone to clean it and YOU will be paying for it.

Here's another reason. This is a situation where <u>you</u> can play the law of averages and win. Do you remember me telling you that being a landlord is a business? Once you move out, your landlord wants to re-rent the apartment. And trust me on this, the last thing he wants to do is track you down to clean grease off the side of the stove. So chances are pretty good that your landlord will not take you up on your offer but it <u>will make you look good</u> for offering.

If you do end up in court about your security deposit you want to be able to show the judge that you did everything you could to leave your apartment clean and in a state of good repair. Your goal here is to protect your security deposit and to do this you need to make yourself look good.

Here's the final reason, if your landlord makes deductions from your deposit for cleaning or repairs and <u>doesn't</u> give you a chance to fix the problem, then, in court, you can put it back on your landlord. And you can let him explain to the judge exactly why you weren't given an opportunity to remedy the problem.

<u>HANDLING CLEANING AND DAMAGES</u>

It is possible that the landlord may find something in the apartment that either needs to be cleaned better or repaired. It should be said that whatever it is that the landlord finds wrong with your apartment, you do NOT have to agree with it. Additionally, you do not have to clean it or even repair it if you don't want to. But at least if you offer, you have the option.

I recommend that you go back and fix whatever it is that the landlord found deficient. Be it cleaning something again, or making a repair. Do it and take pictures of it. If you end up in court, it will show your good faith effort.

TALKING TO THE LANDLORD

So you dropped off your keys, you gave the landlord your request/demand for your security deposit, and you requested to correct any deficiencies. If you have any questions for the landlord, now is the time to ask. At this point, you have done everything that you can to protect your security deposit and if you have no outstanding bills related to your apartment you should get your full security deposit back.

PART FIVE

ELEVEN

GETTING YOUR SECURITY DEPOSIT BACK

* * *

A word of caution: If you are starting here, you may think that you can just read this chapter and get your security deposit back. That would be a mistake.

Actually, this is the gravy chapter. The work is already done.

Sorry, but you will find that there is no easy way to avoid the previous steps without some effect, most likely devastating, on the return of your security deposit.

* * *

Once you have come this far you've done everything that you can to protect your security deposit and getting it back is easy. All you have to do is wait. As easy as it sounds, this can be a difficult step for some people.

As much as tenants would like their security deposit back as soon as they move out, it usually doesn't work that way. (I'll give you a little window into the WHY? For me, I am usually waiting for final bills, like sewer bills that are sent from the city.)

The amount of time that the landlord has to return a security deposit varies from state to state. In Wisconsin, the law allows your landlord twenty-one days from the time you vacate the premises to return your security deposit to your last known address. Some landlords will take the full twenty-one days and others will return your deposit sooner. Check the lease for your state law regarding the time frame to return your security deposit.

PENALTIES FOR NOT RETURNING YOUR DEPOSIT

State governments are becoming more responsive to landlord/tenant problems concerning security deposits. There are laws in most states that penalize the landlord for not returning the security deposit or informing the tenant why it is being withheld. The penalties are in the form of money. Tenants can receive *double* or even *triple damages*. So, relax, trust me, your landlord is well aware of the law. Chances are good that you will hear from your landlord.

THE TIME IS UP

You have waited the full twenty-one days. You have not gotten your security deposit back and you have not heard from your landlord. What should you do?

Call your landlord and ask about your security deposit. Some good communication at this point can go a long way. If it has been more than twenty-one days from the time you vacated the premises **and** you gave the landlord your forwarding address, unless there is some unusual circumstance involved, you should have heard from your landlord. At this point, your landlord better have a good explanation.

PROBLEMS WITH YOUR SECURITY DEPOSIT

A letter arrives from your landlord containing a check for part of your security deposit or it may be a letter itemizing why you aren't getting your security deposit back.

You were expecting the full return of your security deposit. This letter will make you angry, and rightfully so. It is your money. You want it. You need it. And you have been waiting patiently to get it.

Your first thought may be to call your landlord and yell, swear and maybe even threaten him. It is okay to be angry but the first thing you need to do is process the anger. Step back, take time to think this through but do not call your landlord until you've had time to digest all of the information in the letter.

Take the opportunity to look at the deductions. What dollar amount is deducted and why? Is this a legitimate deduction? Do you have pictures to show that this deduction is unwarranted? If the deduction was for damage or cleaning, do you have pictures that tell a different story?

Once you have had time to process the information in the letter and are clear with your thoughts, call your landlord for a better explanation. Ask him why he made these deductions. Let him know that you disagree and tell him <u>why</u> you disagree with the deductions. Why you think that they are inaccurate or unfair.

It is always a good first step to try to resolve the differences with your landlord. If you find that you cannot come to some type of agreement, at least now you know you'll have a fight on your hands to get your security deposit back.

SUMMARY AND SOLUTION

When your landlord withholds your security deposit or makes deductions and returns only a portion of your deposit, you will not be happy. But, if you've been with me since the beginning of this book, you will realize that this is what we have been preparing for all along.

We started protecting your security deposit before you even moved in and extended that protection throughout your tenancy. At "Moving Out" time everything was done to move out correctly so that you could get your security deposit back.

So, all along while you thought that you would have no problem getting your security deposit back, you were also preparing for the worst case scenario - the landlord keeping it or keeping part of it.

Now, with all the preparation that you have done, at least you do have some options. You do not have to walk away and forget your deposit. You have adequate documentation. You protected your security deposit in every way you could. At this point, you may have to take your landlord to court to get your security deposit back.

In Chapter Twelve we will discuss making the decision to go to Small Claims Court.

TWELVE

The Decision To Go To Small Claims Court

When your landlord makes excessive or wrongful deductions from your security deposit you have the right to challenge them. While going to Small Claims Court is an option, there are other things that you can try first.

COMMUNITY RESOURCES

As I said in the last chapter, you should attempt to resolve this matter with your landlord. See if you can come to some type of agreement. If there is any hope of settling this issue with your landlord you can avoid the time and expense of court action.

If there is no way that you are able to come to an agreement, see what other resources are available in your community. Try the following:

1. Tenant organizations - If there is a tenant organization in your area, contact them. You would be surprised how much these organizations can accomplish. Look online to find an organization in your area.
2. Legal Action Wisconsin - if you qualify, legal aid can help you. Each case is different and they will determine to what extent they

can help you. I have seen a Legal Action Attorney in court fighting for the tenant in a security deposit issue. Seeking their help can be worth the effort.
3. Consumer Hotline / Consumer Protection Agency – every state has an agency that protects consumers. You may also be able to submit a complaint online. When you contact these agencies they will investigate to determine if the landlord is violating the law.

DECIDING HOW TO PROCEED

Get as much information and guidance as you can from these sources. You may find that others agree that the deductions are unwarranted and that you would have a good chance of getting a favorable decision if you proceed with a court case.

If you have pictures and documentation that show that the deductions are inaccurate or false, you have the right to the return of your security deposit. While you and your landlord may disagree on these issues, this is exactly why we have a Small Claims Court, to settle these types of problems.

While Small Claims cases are considered to be lawsuits, a Small Claims trial is designed to provide an inexpensive and speedy method of settling minor claims. Small Claims Courts will only hear those cases that involve claims under a certain dollar amount. If you plan to pursue a small claims case, check the Wisconsin State Statutes (or Statutes for your state). This information can also be found at the Small Claims Court website for your county. Some states allow attorneys in Small Claim Court while others do not.

YOUR DECISION

Once you gather information you will be able to decide if it is worth pursuing a Small Claims Case. If you tried to settle this with your landlord without success, and the deductions were of a sizable amount of money that you feel is worth pursuing, then your next step would be to send your landlord a certified letter.

Summarize your conversation regarding the security deposit deductions and let him know <u>what you think would be fair</u>. If you think that returning your full deposit would be fair, say that.

Tell him that you have documentation that his deductions are incorrect or false (if that is the case). You do not have to go into detail about the exact documentation that you have. Conclude your letter by saying that you would like your money refunded, and if he does not do so that you intend to proceed with legal action.

In reality, you are not required to send your landlord a letter notifying him of your plans, but it might be worth the effort. It might be just enough of a push that he will decide that it is easier to settle this issue with you than it would be to go to court. Remember that saying, *"The squeaky wheel gets the grease?"*

GOING TO SMALL CLAIMS COURT

Have you ever been to Small Claims Court before? Making the decision to proceed to Small Claims Court can be scary, especially for someone who has never been there before. While using Small Claims Court is the way to pursue your security deposit, many tenants hesitate to use the system.

Let's consider their concerns:

1. **Tenants feel that they will be in unfamiliar territory.**

    If you have never been to Small Claims Court before then, yes, it is true, you will be in unfamiliar territory. But I will let you in on a little secret: there are some landlords who have never been to Small Claims Court, either. So, it will be unfamiliar territory to them as well and going into court they will feel just as lost as you do.

    The landlords who have been to Small Claims Court do have experience on their side. However, this is not a good reason to avoid Small Claims Court. We learn by doing and we become experienced by doing. And there are things that you can do to offset the landlord's advantage. *If he indeed has one.*

In fact, if you have followed the steps in this book you will have the proof, documentation, and evidence that you need in court. You will be ready. *That should help level the playing field.* You have all the benefits of what I have learned over the past twenty-plus-years.

2. **Tenants do not think that they can win in Small Claims Court.** This is really the most important issue. If you start with an *"I can't win"* attitude, eventually it will become a self-fulfilling prophecy. Then, you will not only lose, but you will say, "See, I told you that I couldn't win."

    A negative attitude will work against you every time. If you honestly feel that you cannot win, then you better examine the situation. Do you have the evidence to show that your claim (what you are saying), is correct? Do you think that you are right and that you deserve your security deposit back? Do you think that you deserve to win?

    If the answer is **YES!** to these questions, then maybe you are just <u>apprehensive</u> about the whole Small Claims Court process. That is called *fear*. And it is very normal. So just acknowledge that this <u>is</u> all new and the fear that you are feeling is normal. Suck it up. Be brave! You <u>do</u> deserve to get your security deposit back. So, march into court believing that you not only <u>deserve</u> to win, but that you <u>can</u> win. The best way to keep this positive attitude is to be prepared.

    In court, these feelings of uncertainty will pop up again. Normalize the whole situation as much as possible. Tell yourself that this situation is tough (because it is) and it is stressful (because it is) but the court process will not last forever. Under the circumstances, these feelings are normal. BUT you still deserve to win.

    With all of that being said, even with the right attitude there is still the possibility that you will not win. But at least with a positive attitude you will have a fighting chance.

    In reality, since the deductions were already made from your security deposit, you have already lost the money. So, by going to

Small Claims Court, you have nothing to lose and everything to gain. You are going for justice and for your money. Taking it step-by-step, learning as much as you can and by being prepared, you can do it. The good news about Small Claims Court is that you definitely do have a chance of winning.

3. **Tenants feel that it is easier to forget about their security deposit and just walk away.**
Yes, it is easier to walk away.

If you have never been to Small Claims Court and you have no idea how to prepare a court case it can be very stressful and intimidating. Just forgetting about your security deposit does seem like the logical thing to do. And who can really blame you?

If the dollar amount of your claim is small, it may not be worth your time and effort to go after it. In this case, it would be easier to walk away. But forgetting about it would not be an option. Whatever the dollar amount is… whatever the disagreement is… **if** you decide to walk away, use it as a learning experience to help you avoid such a deduction in the future. Going to Small Claims Court is not on anyone's top ten list of fun things to do. But sometimes it becomes a necessary evil.

Landlords need to know that tenants are willing to stand up to them and that unfair, illegal, and excessive deductions will not be tolerated. The areas where you feel that the odds are against you can be overcome. Besides, what is your alternative? You don't want to encourage your landlord to keep security deposits… *particularly yours*… and you certainly don't want to forfeit your deposit every time you move. When your landlord is unjust with you, *get angry*, *get determined*, and *go for justice*.

Once you have been to court you will have what is called *experience*. In the future you will know what to expect in court, how to prepare, and taking each step will be easier. I recommend that once you have this knowledge, join a tenant's organization and give back. Help others.

THIRTEEN

GOING TO SMALL CLAIMS COURT

Once you decide to go to Small Claims Court another barrage of questions will hit you. Where is Small Claims Court? How do I start a Small Claims Case? Should I hire an attorney? What if the landlord has an attorney? What is Small Claims Court like? How do I prepare a Case? Or even present a Case?

WHERE IS SMALL CLAIMS COURT?

Small Claims Courts are local, usually in your county, if not in your city. Which makes them easy to find. They are said to be quick, cheap, and fair. They are also informal. The procedures are not as rigid and you can present a successful case without an attorney's know-how.

To find the Small Claims Court in your county, I suggest that you start by looking online. Use your search engine and type in: <u>the name of your county</u>, (followed by) Small Claims Court. This should give you a number of sites to choose from and a wealth of knowledge to help you learn about the whole process of going to Small Claims Court, including the necessary forms, the instructions, and information on preparing and presenting your case.

WHEN DO I START A SMALL CLAIMS CASE?

When you have had unfair or unwarranted deductions made from your security deposit and you have exhausted all of your other options, including attempts to settle this with your landlord without success, it is time to think about starting a small claims case.

SHOULD I HIRE AN ATTORNEY?

This is an important question. The whole idea of Small Claims Court is to keep justice simple and eliminate the necessity of having an attorney. In a Small Claims case, it may cost you more money to hire an attorney than you could ever hope to win in court. So keep in mind the amount of money you are seeking to recover in court.

At this point, you may want to consider <u>consulting</u> with an attorney. Ask about charges in advance so that you don't end up with a huge bill. Take your manila envelope with your documentation and any communication you've had with your landlord. Ask the attorney to review your paperwork because you want to know if you have a case worth pursuing.

Going to court to get your security deposit back is an emotionally charging issue. You are angry at your landlord, and rightfully so. But do not let this cloud your thinking when you talk to an attorney.

Attorneys know the court process and their advice will be worth the price you pay for the consultation. When you talk to an attorney, keep in mind that you're <u>asking for their professional advice</u> and you are <u>not</u> there looking for someone to just *take your side*.

WHAT IF THE LANDLORD HAS AN ATTORNEY?

If your landlord has an attorney in court, it may intimidate you and even make you wonder if you really have a chance of winning. This will feel like a real disadvantage to you. Somehow, it does seem unfair when one side is represented by an attorney in Small Claims Court and the other is not. Attorneys do have experience and education on their side.

Just remember that Small Claims Court judges do not expect the people involved in disputes to act like they have a law degree. Through experience, judges can get the facts of the case from both sides. The presence of an attorney may only help the process along, at least on one side. You should also know that being represented by an attorney is no guarantee that you will win.

I witnessed a Small Claims Court case where the side represented by the attorney <u>did not win</u>. While attorneys do have education and experience they cannot change the evidence involved in the case. When it comes right down to it, the facts, the evidence, and how you present it is what will make or break your case. If you have a good case with strong evidence, your landlord's attorney cannot change that. <u>Believe in your case</u>.

<u>WHAT IS SMALL CLAIMS COURT LIKE?</u>

The words that come to my mind are quiet and serious. If you have never been in a courtroom, or never been to Small Claims Court, the first time can be a little scary.

Getting a preview of the whole court experience before your court case would be beneficial. Take a friend with you if needed. Sit in on a few court cases and listen. Watch the procedures and make it a learning experience. If possible, sit in on a landlord/tenant case and see what happens. Get acquainted with the surroundings. Then, when your court day comes, you will feel more at ease. You will know where to go and what to expect.

The last thing that you want to do on your court date is to wander around the court house trying to find the courtroom and then end up racing in late. You will feel hurried, flustered, and uncomfortable.

<u>HOW DO I PREPARE AND PRESENT A CASE?</u>

Start online, again using the search engine. Type in your state, and then: preparing a Small Claims Court Case, or, how to prepare a Small Claims

Court Case. Be creative and you will end up with a lot of helpful information and some good examples.

THE JUDGE

Some people believe that the Judge is on the side of the landlord and that you (the tenant) don't have a chance from the start. Other people believe that the Judge sides with the underdog (the tenant), because it is human nature to do so.

Everyone has the right to their own opinion. But, in all reality, the Judge is a professional. He is both educated and experienced. Every day he has the responsibility of making decisions that effect the lives of the people in his courtroom.

The thing that you need to know about the Judge is this, when you come into his courtroom, the Judge has not heard the details from either side of your court case. <u>He is the neutral person there</u>. His job is to hear both sides.

So, despite the fact that you may be upset and angry at your landlord, you need to set those feelings aside. The things that you <u>do not want to do</u> are: interrupt, yell, swear at your landlord, call your landlord names or tell the Judge what a terrible person your landlord is.

Rather, dress appropriately, be respectful, and go into the courtroom with a positive attitude. Believe in your case and present your side of the case and your evidence <u>to the Judge</u>. Again, remember... you are there to present your case to the Judge. He is the person who will be deciding the outcome of your case.

THE DECISION

When all of the evidence and testimony has been presented the Judge will make his decision. In thinking about the Judge's decision, you may be thinking in terms of *winning* or *losing*.

ABOUT LOSING

It takes a huge amount of courage and effort just to go to Small Claims Court and present your case. If you lose your court case it will be emotionally difficult. When you lose you may feel like the Judge was not fair, that he did not listen to your side of the case or even consider your evidence. You may even think that the Judge <u>really was</u> on the landlord's side and that you did not have a chance from the start. These are all common feelings.

ABOUT WINNING

When you win your court case you will have the thrill of victory. And the stress, strain, and money involved will have been worth it. When you win, the overall common feeling is that the Judge was fair and justice was served... and by golly, our Justice System does work after all!

ABOUT WINNING AND LOSING

There is good news about the decisions that the Judge makes in Small Claims Court regarding landlord/tenant cases. Sometimes it is not a winner-takes-all contest. If several items of cleaning and damage are part of the court case, it is possible that the Judge will allow some of the deductions and disallow others. If this is the Judge's decision (and the case result), then it allows both parties to emerge somewhat victorious and feel like justice has been (at least partially) served.

SUMMARY

Whether you win, lose, or salvage a partial victory, going to court is always a learning experience. The most meaningful lessons in life are the ones that are the hardest learned. Your first time in court will be the most difficult. Once it is over, you will then take on the distinguished title of *"Experienced"* and each court appearance after that will be easier;

whether it is your case, or you are there in a supportive role to others. Remember to take what you have learned and give back.

Our Justice System is far from perfect, but it is still the best one we have. While justice may not be dispensed one-hundred-percent of the time, there is always the hope and possibility that it will be in your case.

FINAL THOUGHTS

Congratulations on making it to the end of the book. You now have an understanding of the complete tenancy process. You also have the step-by-step instructions you need to protect your security deposit.

Remember that time is a huge factor when you make the decision to move. I have found that <u>not</u> planning ahead or allotting enough time for your move are the biggest stumbling blocks that tenants seem to encounter. Things get left undone that result in security deposit deductions. So, plan ahead because with all of the other demands on your life, you only have so much energy.

If your landlord makes unfair or excessive deductions from your security deposit you have pictures and documentation that will enable you to put your case together and present it in Small Claims Court. You can do this. Believe in yourself and your case.

Best regards,
Sandy

FORMS

TENANCY CHECKLIST FORM

TENANCY CHECKLIST

Place a check mark next to each item as you put it in the envelope.

_____ 1. Keys (number of keys received) _____
_____ 2. Rent receipts
_____ 3. Security Deposit receipt
_____ 4. Copy of Lease Agreement
_____ 5. Copy of charges made to the last tenant's security deposit
_____ 6. Smoke Detector Agreement
_____ 7. Carbon Monoxide Detector Agreement
_____ 8. Check-In Form
_____ 9. Agreement to Electronic Delivery of Documents
_____ 10. Other _____
_____ 11. Other _____

REPAIR/CLEANING AGREEMENT FORM:

REPAIR/CLEANING AGREEMENT

Date_____

_____ tenant at: _____ agrees to do the following list of repairs/cleaning at the rental address _____ in exchange for the $_____ security deposit.

1. _____
2. _____
3. _____
4. _____

The landlord agrees to obtain/pay for the materials and the tenant will provide the labor.

The repairs completion date: _____

tenant _____

landlord _____

Combined **CHECK-IN CHECKLIST/DAMAGE INFORMATION REQUEST FORM**:

CHECK-IN CHECKLIST/DAMAGE INFORMATION REQUEST

Address of rental unit: _____
Name of Tenant(s): _____
Move in date: _____

Please check the condition of the following items within seven (7) days of tenancy:

-kitchen appliances
-sink/toilet
-tub/shower
-light fixtures
-walls and woodwork
-doors
-ceilings
-windows
-floors
-carpeting

Please note the general condition of the apartment and let us know about any damage or problems that we should be aware of.

Damage Information Request
☐ I/we request a list of physical damages or defects that were charged to the previous tenant's security deposit.

_____   _____
Tenant signature   Date

CHECK-OUT CHECKLIST FORM:

CHECK-OUT CHECKLIST

Address of rental unit: _____
Name of Tenant(s): _____
Last date of tenancy: _____

Please check the condition of the following items:

-kitchen appliances
-sink/toilet
-tub/shower
-light fixtures
-walls and woodwork
-doors
-ceilings
-windows
-floors
-carpeting

Notes: _____
_____
_____
_____
_____
_____
_____

_____
Tenant signature

_____   _____
Tenant signature   Date

Simple 30-DAY NOTICE OF INTENT TO VACATE PREMISES FORM:
30-DAY NOTICE OF INTENT TO VACATE PREMISES

Date: _____

This is my 30-Day notice that I will be vacating the premises at: _____ _____ on or before: _____.

The apartment will be left clean, in good condition and I will remove my personal possessions. I will return the key on or before: _____

My forwarding address is: _____

If you have any questions you may contact me at: _____

Sincerely,

_____
Tenant

30-DAY NOTICE WITH DEMAND FOR SECURITY DEPOSIT FORM:

30-DAY NOTICE OF INTENT TO VACATE PREMISES

Date: _____
Address: _____

This is my 30-Day Notice that I will be vacating the premises on or before: _____ I am giving you the proper notice that is required by our lease agreement.

The apartment will be left clean and in good condition. I will remove my personal possessions and I will return the key on or before: _____

I would like my security deposit back as soon as possible because I will need it for my new apartment.

    The forwarding address for the return of my security deposit is: _____

If you have any questions you may contact me at: _____

Sincerely,

_____
Tenant

Optional DEMAND FOR SECURITY DEPOSIT FORM:

DEMAND FOR SECURITY DEPOSIT

Date _____
Dear _____ (Landlord)

Per our lease agreement, I have given you a 30-Day Notice. I moved all of my possessions out of the apartment at _____ (address) as of the above date.

    I left the apartment clean and in good repair. When you inspect the apartment if something is not as clean as expected, or you believe that there is damage I would like the opportunity to remedy the situation.

    I am returning _____ keys with this notice.

    If you have any questions or concerns you can contact me at this number: _____

My new address is: _____

    I would like my security deposit returned as soon as possible so that I can use it at my new apartment.

Sincerely,

_____

(Tenant)

TENANT RESOURCES

WISCONSIN
Tenant Resource Center: www.tenantresourcecenter.org

RESOURCES BY STATE

ALABAMA
Alabama Legal Help: alabamalegalhelp.org

ARIZONA
Arizona Tenants Advocates: Arizonatenants.com

CALIFORNIA
Tenants Together: tenantstogether.org
California Coalition for Rural Housing: calruralhousing.org
Housing Rights Center: housingrightscenter.org
San Francisco Tenants Union: sftu.org
Housing Rights Committee of SF: hrcsf.org
Coalition for Economic Survival: cesinaction.org

ILLINOIS
Metro Tenants Organization: tenants-rights.org
Illinois Tenants Union: www.tenant.org
Center for Renters' Rights: www.renters-rights.com

IOWA
Home, Inc: homeincdsm.org

KANSAS
Housing and Credit Counseling, Inc: www.khlaac.ks.gov/resources/housing-credit-counseling

KENTUCKY
Homeless and Housing Coalition of Kentucky: www.hhck.org

MAINE
Portland Tenants Union: Portlandtenantsunion.org

MARYLAND
Maryland Legal Aid Bureau, Inc: www.mdlab.org

MASSACHUSETTS
Mass Legal Services: masslegalservices.org

MICHIGAN
Legal Services of Eastern Michigan: www.lsem-mi.org
Michigan Tenant Counseling Program

MINNESOTA
Minnesota Tenants Union: minnesotatenantsunion.org

HOME Line: homelinemn.org

NEW JERSEY
New Jersey Tenants Organization: njtenantsorg.homestead.com

NEW YORK
NY Tenants & Neighbors: tandn.org

NORTH CAROLINA
Greensboro Housing Coalition: greensborohousingcoalition.com

OHIO
Cleveland Tenants Organization: clevelandtenants.org

OREGON
Community Alliance of Tenants: oregoncat.org

PENNSYLVANIA
Tenants Union Representative Network: www.rturn.net

TEXAS
Texas Tenants' Union: txtenants.org

UTAH
Crossroads Urban Center: crossroadsurbancenter.org

WASHINGTON
Tenants Union of Washington State: tenantsunion.org

NATIONAL RESOURCES
HUD.gov

ABOUT THE AUTHOR

Sandy lives in Wisconsin and has been a landlord for more than twenty years. She has a Master of Science Degree from UW-Madison.

Through her years as a landlord Sandy could see recurring situations where tenants got tripped up and struggled with security deposit issues. She wrote this book to help tenants understand how to protect their security deposit during the rental process so that they are able to get it back when they move on to their next apartment.

ONE LAST THING...

If this guide has been useful for you, please post a review to let others know. Your support and acknowledgement are greatly appreciated.